Tracing Arachne's Web

Copyright 2001 by Kristin M. Mapel Bloomberg. This work is licensed under a modified Creative Commons Attribution-Noncommercial-No Derivative Works 3.0 Unported License. To view a copy of this license, visit *http://creativecommons.org/licenses/by-nc-nd/3.0/*. You are free to electronically copy, distribute, and transmit this work if you attribute authorship. *However, all printing rights are reserved by the University Press of Florida (http://www.upf.com). Please contact UPF for information about how to obtain copies of the work for print distribution.* You must attribute the work in the manner specified by the author or licensor (but not in any way that suggests that they endorse you or your use of the work). For any reuse or distribution, you must make clear to others the license terms of this work. Any of the above conditions can be waived if you get permission from the University Press of Florida. Nothing in this license impairs or restricts the author's moral rights.

Florida A&M University, Tallahassee
Florida Atlantic University, Boca Raton
Florida Gulf Coast University, Ft. Myers
Florida International University, Miami
Florida State University, Tallahassee
University of Central Florida, Orlando
University of Florida, Gainesville
University of North Florida, Jacksonville
University of South Florida, Tampa
University of West Florida, Pensacola

# Tracing Arachne's Web

Myth and Feminist Fiction

Kristin M. Mapel Bloomberg

University Press of Florida
Gainesville · Tallahassee · Tampa · Boca Raton
Pensacola · Orlando · Miami · Jacksonville · Ft. Myers

Copyright 2001 by Kristin M. Mapel Bloomberg

All rights reserved

06 05 04 03 02 01   6 5 4 3 2 1

Library of Congress Cataloging-in-Publication Data
Bloomberg, Kristin M. Mapel, 1969–
Tracing Arachne's web: myth and feminist fiction / Kristin M. Mapel Bloomberg.
p. cm.
Includes bibliographical references (p. ) and index.
ISBN 978-1-61610-107-7
1. Feminist fiction, American—History and criticism. 2. American fiction—Women authors—History and criticism. 3. Feminism and literature—United States—History. 4. Women and literature—United States—History. 5. Mythology, Classical, in literature. 6. Women—Mythology. 7. Myth in literature. I. Title.
PS374.F45 B58 2001
813.009'9287—dc21   2001027354

The University Press of Florida is the scholarly publishing agency for the State University System of Florida, comprising Florida A&M University, Florida Atlantic University, Florida Gulf Coast University, Florida International University, Florida State University, University of Central Florida, University of Florida, University of North Florida, University of South Florida, and University of West Florida.

University Press of Florida
15 Northwest 15th Street
Gainesville, FL 32611–2079
http://www.upf.com

*This book is dedicated to all of my "literary mothers" who have assisted me with the birth of my very own book.*

# Contents

1. Tracing Arachne's Web: Mythic Methods and Femin(ine)ist Fictions  1

2. Occulted Words and Mythic Worlds  16

3. Unraveling Demeter's Garden: Demeter and Persephone in the Works of Sarah Orne Jewett and Emma D. Kelley-Hawkins  26

4. Aphrodite's Fall: Aphrodite, Undine, and Andromeda in the Works of Onoto Watanna, Alice Dunbar-Nelson, and Edith Wharton  53

5. Hekate's Queendom of the Damned: Djuna Barnes's *Nightwood*  87

One Thread of Arachne's Web  106

Notes  109

Bibliography  115

Index  123

# 1

## Tracing Arachne's Web
*Mythic Methods and Femin(ine)ist Fictions*

\* From classical mythology we hear the story of Arachne: mortal daughter of a famous dye-maker, and a brilliant mistress of the loom who entered into a contest with Fate-Weaver Athena. During the course of the contest, Arachne weaves a perfect tapestry depicting the scandals of the gods, thus sending her immortal competitor into a rage. Athena then strikes Arachne with her shuttle, transforming the young woman into a spider; thus, Arachne is left to practice her craft without danger of outdoing the goddess again. Certainly, this myth is a not-so-subtle parable of the dangers of the student outdoing the teacher or of the underling outperforming the master, but the myth is usually told from the point of view of one sympathetic to those in power—the gods. So what can Arachne's story reveal when the story is told from her point of view?

To understand Arachne's point of view, it is important to comprehend the diversity of Arachne's symbolic and metaphorical meanings. For example, her skill in weaving tapestries is also symbolic of her skill in weaving stories—her myth tells how her final work narrated in thread the scandals of the gods. Accordingly, the figure of Arachne calls to mind a metaphor for women writing, one that is embedded in her name itself. In *Lady of the Beasts,* Buffie Johnson explains the etymological roots of Arachne's name and her symbolic creature: "The word *spider* comes from the Old English *spinan,* meaning 'to spin.' The modern word *spinster,* unwed woman, arises from the ancient idea that the spinners of fate were virgin goddesses who spun not only human life but the fate of the world. In Sanskrit, to sew is *siv,* the same root as thread. It is preserved in the Latin *suo;* in English, 'to sew.' Another Sanskrit root is *nah;* from it stems Latin *neo* and *necto* 'spider,' literally 'the wool spinner.' *Rak* in Greek corresponds to the Greek word meaning 'to stitch together,' 'to weave'; hence Arachne, a fine weaver in Greek myth" (210). Johnson further demonstrates that the spider is an intermediary or liminal figure because she weaves her web in the air yet anchors it to the ground; hence, she is neither fully a creature of the sky nor of the earth, but a part of both.

Like Arachne, the women I study here—Sarah Orne Jewett, Emma D. Kelley-Hawkins, Onoto Watanna, Edith Wharton, Alice Dunbar-Nelson, and Djuna Barnes—are also intermediary or liminal figures. It seems no two scholars can agree upon whether writers in this group are a part of the traditional canon of American literature or outside of it; whether they are modernist writers or writing fiction that lies outside the scope of modernism; whether they are true feminist writers or too sentimental, traditional, romantic, regional, or nihilistic to be feminist. As a result of these characteristics, then, the liminal figure of Arachne is the perfect ruling metaphor for the women writers analyzed in this study.

In addition to her appearance in classical mythology, Arachne also appears in Native American religious myths in the figure of Spider Grandmother or Thought Woman who also weave stories; however, Spider Grandmother's power is even more significant than Arachne's because she has the power to create life itself. Marta Weigle explains that for Pueblo peoples, Spider Grandmother is a "supreme being who creates everything by thinking, dreaming, naming, and ritual singing" (346). In another context, Pueblo writer Leslie Marmon Silko narrates Spider-Woman's story:

Ts'its'tsi'nako, Thought-Woman
is sitting in her room
and whatever she thinks about
appears.

She thought of her sisters,
Nau'ts'ity'i and I'tcts'ity'i,
and together they created the Universe

this world
and the four worlds below.

Thought-Woman, the spider,
named things and
as she named them
they appeared.

she is sitting in her room
thinking of a story now. (1)

Silko's poem tells the story of the mythological spider who creates the Universe by thinking it into being, just as Thought-Woman or Spider Grandmother weave the stories that tell the world into existence. As a result, when set beside that of Spider Grandmother or Thought-Woman, the story of Arachne can be re-seen as an empowering woman's mythology that can revise the perspective of a somewhat silent classical Arachne.

Arachne is a powerful metaphor for the study of women writers who, like Spider Grandmother, think up new worlds in the stories that they spin, and who, like Arachne, dare to challenge the establishment by comparing themselves to it. But as Jane Caputi observes, Arachne's story reveals that this can be a dangerous and radical enterprise, because when women "foray into the realm traditionally forbidden to our sex—the realm of the sacred storytellers, symbol and myth-makers—we participate in the creative powers of Thought Woman, employing thinking, naming and willing as forms of power exercised consciously and/or intuitively in the creation of the world(s) we inhabit" (427). Like Spider Grandmother Arachne, the women writers studied here foray into realms traditionally forbidden to their sex in order to weave new fictional worlds and create new female and feminist mythologies.

All of the women I study here create narratives that employ both modernist literary techniques and classical or mythic tropes; however, my goal is not to use my analysis of these women writers to create an ultimate definition of either literary myth or literary modernism, nor is this a comparative study of classical and contemporary texts. Instead, my intention is to explore literature that exists on the margins of both modernism and myth in order to provide a provocative, albeit partial, rereading of all three. While so-called high modernists such as Eliot, Joyce, Yeats, and Pound all have well-documented connections to myth, others writing along the historical and formal margins of modernism have significant relationships to myth as well. These include the women writers studied here. Moreover, because this study deals with the authors' manipulation of images from popular culture, identifying the specific textual sources of myth these authors read is less important than recognizing the fact that these culturally and racially diverse authors share general allusions to figures of classical mythology as familiar archetypal and iconographic images that are part of a common cultural language in fin-de-siècle America. For example, because myth is part of a general cultural tradition shared through narrative, it is unlikely that these writers were specifically influenced by—or that a critic can claim that they were influenced by—a single textual source. Indeed, the sources these authors may have drawn upon might include not only traditional classical texts such as Homer, but also visual, musical, theatrical, and poetic texts presented by turn-of-the-twentieth century painters, composers, and authors. It is difficult to determine if these writers studied the primary works of classical writers—indeed, it may be irrelevant, because these women writers were sensitive not to the staid intellectual (and masculine) culture of warmly paneled lecture halls, but to the vibrant and dynamic popular culture of theater, public art, women's magazines, and fashion.

An examination of these late-nineteenth- and early-twentieth-century women writers in juxtaposition with myth—which is one of the crucial threads of high modernism—creates an engaging dialectical lens with which to view a period of literature written by women. Moreover, Ann Ardis observes that "to attend to marginality, to narrate a shifting limit between the New Woman novel and high modernism, means challenging the familiar periodization of modern literary history" (5). In the spirit of Ardis's design, my goal is to similarly pick up a thread woven throughout so-called high modernism, to follow it along the fringes of modernism, and to see how it is interlaced with the work of late-nineteenth- and early-twentieth-century women writers—some lesser known, some very familiar. Consequently, my specific intention is to trace the path of one thread within the tapestry of modernism: namely, these women authors' weaving of mythic and occult elements into their work. In doing so, it is possible to show how these women put to early use a modernist "mythical method," to use T. S. Eliot's famous phrase. Moreover, I hope to demonstrate how these women reshaped mythic themes and occult tropes in their semiotic narratives to create a liberatory exploration of women's position under patriarchy and the limitations of women's words.

As readers have learned from any number of histories about the late nineteenth and early twentieth century, modernism as an artistic, historical, literary, or social period is characterized by its multiplicity: symbolism, impressionism, imagism, vorticism, futurism, expressionism, dadaism, and surrealism. Similarly, it is interpreted through the form of the novel, poem, prose poem, free verse, theatrical production, journalism, essay, and manifesto. It is a literature by whites, blacks, Asian Americans, Chicanos, and American Indians; by women, men, lesbians, bisexuals, and gays; who were also Christians, Jews, protestants, agnostics, atheists, goddess worshippers, mystics, gypsies, mediums, rationalists, fascists, communists, anarchists, and individualists. It was written by artists who were working-class, middle-class, upper-class, classically educated, self-educated, or educated by life experience—and by people who rejected simple definitions of gender, race, class, status, and intellectual ability. My point here is that modernism is a mix, a movement of an artistic social community that allowed *everyone* to rub elbows with each other at one time or another.

Our own turn of the century has seen reconsiderations of the fin de siècle of one hundred years ago, resulting in provocative academic studies such as Ann Ardis's *New Women, New Novels: Feminism and Early Modernism* (1990), Elizabeth Ammons's *Conflicting Stories: American Women Writers at the Turn into the Twentieth Century* (1992), and Martha J. Cutter's *Unruly Tongue: Identity and Voice in American Women's Writing, 1850–1930* (1999). Like Ardis, Ammons, and Cutter, I have purposefully grouped together late-nineteenth- and early-twentieth-century American women writers to consider some of the multiplicities of gender, race, class, age, regionalism, narrative form, and philosophy. As these critics demonstrate, the period from around 1880 through that of World War I saw great social, political, and cultural changes for American women, changes reflected in the works produced by turn-of-the-twentieth-century women writers who explored, analyzed, critiqued, embraced, or rejected the verities of their positions in American society.

Grouping together women writing around the turn of the twentieth century intersects with questions about periodizing American literary history itself. Like Ammons, I believe that examining a historical cross section of women writers in this period can contribute "to the ongoing revision of the still-popular modern thesis that the nation's 'best' and most characteristic literature is antirealistic" (*Conflicting Stories* ix). With Ammons, I believe that splitting literary history into a hierarchical linear progression from naturalism and realism at the bottom to experimental modernism at the top only serves to scatter and divide the work of women writers, thus discounting them as primary foci of serious literary study. Instead, I believe it is interestingly productive to examine these writers not in terms of their differences but in terms of their similarities—because that is where their revolutionary power can be exposed.

In this way, it is possible to examine a writer such as Edith Wharton as *both* a realist *and* a modernist, depending upon which textual threads in her works are studied. Viewing women's texts in this way creates a literary history that is more fluid, flexible, and accurate. Certainly, literary realism did not "shut off" in January of a certain year while another period began—these historical changes are more gradual and supple than syllabi typically allow. Moreover, such rigid classifications only serve to isolate writers in an artificial way, discounting the influence of literary works and historical experience on later texts.

With this in mind, my study examines three generations of American women writers in order to soften the lines of women's modernism to examine where the anchor lines of women's modernism might be found. I have organized my analysis of these women writers as others have done (quite) loosely around the historical time period of America's Progressive Era: with the texts of the first generation of writers appearing at the beginning of the era in the latter part of the nineteenth century, the texts of the second generation during the Progressive Era's height through the early twentieth century, and the texts of the third during its decline. Assembling together the fiction produced by women around this period brings into relief an important interval in American fiction wherein the works of these women writers begin to coalesce into a web of recurring, but complicated, themes that focus on issues of liberatory language and authority for women in a drastically changing world. Viewed under this light, a body of work begins to emerge, characterized by what Ammons explains in *Conflicting Stories* as a "shared focus on issues of power: The will to break silence by exposing the connection among institutionalized violence, the sexual exploitations of women, and female muteness; preoccupation with the figure of the woman artist; the need to find union and reunion with the world of one's mother, particularly as one journeyed farther and farther from that world into territory traditionally marked off as forbidden; the corrosion of racism, including and often especially the oppression of women of color by white women; and the difficulty of dealing with multiple discrimination—being an immigrant, being lesbian, being black or Eurasian or Indian" (5). For the women studied here, the power of narrative was to be found in the power of the word as a tool with which to explore the intellectual, psychological, and social isolation of women living under patriarchy. Thus, my study focuses on the interrelatedness of women's social and artistic positions expressed through the magical power of narrative.

The six women writers I have chosen to study—Sarah Orne Jewett, Emma D. Kelley-Hawkins, Onoto Watanna, Alice Dunbar-Nelson, Edith Wharton, and Djuna Barnes—represent three generations of women writers who write within and around the time period known by the literary tag modernism. While writing different fictional styles, these writers are united by the fact that they employ in their works variations of occult and classical myths about women, drawing obliquely on the familiarity, ambiguity, and persuasiveness of the mythic journey from the myths of Demeter and Persephone, Aphrodite, Andromeda, Undine, and Hekate. Furthermore, after seeding their work with mythic images, these writers can deploy them as paradigms for female self-control and power, thus occulting revolutionary plans under tropes of traditional figures.

My understanding of how these works are also modernist is not just a matter of historical period, but one that is inherently tied up in how these works use myth. Generally, theories of myth define it as a special kind of narrative that interprets aspects of the world around us. A quick tour of some of the ideas held about the nature and definition of myth by major scholars underscores the broad-based intellectual, social, and psychological territory of myth. For example, Joseph Campbell argues that myths operate on both the spiritual and physical levels to give people social, individual, and psychological direction. Ernst Cassirer shows how myths are both symbolic and metaphorical, while Mircea Eliade maintains that myths are often stories of creation and origin and sacred in nature. Sir James Frazer argues that myths are prescientific explanations for events in the natural world, while Sigmund Freud explains myths as types of public dreams and Carl Jung shows how myths are manifestations of the human collective unconscious. Northrup Frye limits myths to stories about gods and goddesses or supernatural beings, and Claude Lévi-Strauss believes that myths harbor a discernible structure and that their meaning can be uncovered by linguistic analysis.[1] What ties these descriptions of myth together, Robert W. Brockway explains, is the fact that "all myths are stories" (11).

But before readers become too deeply embroiled in the nature of mythic literature, it is important to examine the specific relationship between myth and modernist narrative. Of course, the most famous essay articulating the intersection of modernism and myth is T. S. Eliot's touchstone analysis entitled "Ulysses, Order, and Myth" (1923). Here Eliot describes the "mythic method" he sees at work in James Joyce's celebrated work of high-modernist fiction, *Ulysses* (1922). Contrasting Joyce's "new" narrative method with simple classical allegory, Eliot explains that "Mr. Joyce's parallel use of the *Odyssey* has a great importance. It has the importance of a scientific discovery. No one else has built a novel upon such a foundation before: it has never before been necessary [...]. In using the myth, in manipulating a continuous parallel between contemporaneity and antiquity, Mr. Joyce is pursuing a method which others must pursue after him" (177). Eliot's statement is relevant to my analysis of Jewett, Kelley-Hawkins, Watanna, Dunbar-Nelson, Wharton, and Barnes for at least two reasons. The first is that the central thesis of my inquiry argues these women authors built their novels upon a literary-mythic foundation more than two decades before Eliot identified this narrative strategy in Joyce's masterwork. The second is that Eliot's specific articulation of the "mythic method" is a useful lens with which to view the works of these women writers.

In the interest of clarity and brevity, I turn for a moment to an analysis of Eliot's theories by Jewel Spears Brooker who identifies in his articulation of the mythic method "a defining feature of this modernism, namely, the tendency to move forward by spiraling back and refiguring the past" (1–2). As Brooker argues, and as I also argue below, an obsession with antiquity is central to writers of the modern era; indeed, Brooker explains, many modernists "insisted that going forward involves going back, that securing the future means redeeming the past" (2). Interestingly, Brooker details how Eliot's philosophy gives shape to a particular thread of modernist literature, in that his emphasis on "intellectual comprehensiveness—specifically, his rejection of synthesis and his insistence on a 'both/and' logic of complementarity—illustrates a foundational pattern in modernist thinking" (3). Brooker identifies this pattern as "a metamorphosis of Hegelian and Marxist dialectic" which "involves a play between opposites that moves forward by spiraling back (a return) and up (a transcendence)" (3). But, Brooker argues, Eliot's philosophical notions surpass Hegel "in resisting linearity, eschewing mentalism, and evading synthesis" (3). Certainly, Eliot found a clear example of moving forward by spiraling back in Joyce's *Ulysses*. Here, Eliot found an example of a narrative method he identifies as one that uses classical allusion as "a way of controlling, of ordering, of giving a shape and a significance to the immense panorama of futility and anarchy which is contemporary history" (Eliot 177).

An important point Brooker makes regarding Eliot's philosophical thought is his "rejection of a binary 'either/or' logic of exclusion and his strenuous insistence on a 'both/and' logic of complementarity" (18). Brooker outlines Eliot's fear of thinking analytically because of the distortion produced by binary logic. As she explains, "By its very nature, analysis takes a person from the unity of immediate experience into the fragmentation of dualism, and, furthermore, analytical thinking tends to lock the thinker into the dualistic mode [. . .]. Feeding on itself, analytical thinking produces the endless list of opposites—subject and object, mind and matter, real and ideal" (17–18). Eliot's eschewal of binary oppositions reveals his distaste for synthesis, as he believed that "the appearance of such dualistic categories inevitably invites further analysis and tempts the thinker toward synthesis or an either/or choice" (18). Thus, Eliot's modernist refusal of synthesis strives to hold both sides of the dualism at once. This is key to Eliot's interpretation of the mythical method in narrative, because it is a thesis that lies within the belief that the antithesis between past and present is false. As Brooker explains, Eliot instead substitutes a complementarity that identifies the past as part of the present, the community as part of the individual, and tradition as part of individual talent. In other words, the bottom line of Eliot's philosophical thought is that analytical thinking supported by hierarchal dualisms is a way of breaking complex things apart—while mythical thinking supported by a philosophy of both/and is a way of putting complex things together. And when viewed from a perspective of decades of work on feminist philosophy and theory, Eliot's theory here can be seen as interestingly feminist.

As Eliot remarks in his essay on *Ulysses,* "Psychology [. . .] ethnology, and *The Golden Bough* have concurred to make possible what was impossible even a few years ago. Instead of narrative method, we may now use the mythical method" (178). But Eliot's specific indebtedness to Sir James Frazer and *The Golden Bough* reveals Eliot's assumptions about the centrality of Frazer's work.[2] One might heed the warning of Elizabeth M. Baeten who cautions, "much of the data utilized in the study of myth are collections made by nineteenth-century white men in their quest to ferret out the unusual or the quaint and to bring Christianity and fealty to Empire to the heathens" (26). Baeten determines that "a certain skepticism must be brought to bear" (26) on texts such as Frazer's and Eliot's and the theories that emanate from them as well. Indeed, that skepticism can include an understanding that while *The Golden Bough* and Eliot's article on *Ulysses* certainly might have had a profound influence on many modernist thinkers, they were not the only influences. Moreover, the possibility exists that Frazer and Eliot identified a thread of thought that had been previously present in intellectual culture. If one were to trace parallels here, it is possible to see that while "scholarly" articulations of myth in the form of the Greek classics or the ethnographic accounts of Frazer's work influenced a cohort of university-educated men, unwritten oral history and folk myth traditions certainly may have influenced writers who did not participate in advanced formal educational training. After all, these myths were circulating in oral tradition before they were transcribed as works for scholarly analysis.

With these cautions in mind, T. S. Eliot's "mythical method" is still useful for structuring a reading of my three generations of modernist women writers. Keeping Eliot's theory in mind, readers remember that the decades preceding and following the turn of the twentieth century were years of great upheaval and change—indeed, this picture of a fragmented and chaotic world is one of the hallmarks of the modernist historical period. Reflecting his historical standpoint, Brooker tells us Eliot believed that "to be true to history, art must reflect the world in which it is produced; and to be true to itself, art must be unified. To meet both of these conditions, art would have to be at once chaotic and unified" (119). Eliot found an answer to this seemingly unsolvable problem in Joyce's use of the mythical method. As Brooker explains, "The mythical method solves the chaos-unity dilemma by allowing the coexistence of surface chaos and subsurface unity. Such unity derives neither from sequence nor from abstractions shared by a culture, but from an abstraction selected by an artist and constructed collaboratively with individual readers" (119). As a result, Eliot's indebtedness to Joyce and Frazer is revealed in the fact that each author "does not assume the existence of a culturally shared myth or abstraction. He brings his own myth and takes special care to keep it always in his reader's mind" (119).

This last point is probably the most important aspect of the narrative process of the mythical method. Indeed, the works of Jewett, Kelley-Hawkins, Watanna, Dunbar-Nelson, Wharton, and Barnes all share the core configuration of the mythical narrative method described by T. S. Eliot. The first is that unity in the texts of these writers is created by invoking an extranarrative wholeness; unity "does not derive from the sequential relation of part to part, either chronologically or logically" (Brooker 120). Instead, this unity is a result of a "reference to an abstraction chosen by the artist and brought to his [or her] work" (120). In the case of the women writers studied here, that abstraction is an oblique reference to female figures in mythology.

In order to be true to its time, a work using Eliot's mythical method "must consist of juxtaposed fragments—fragments of contemporary life, fragments of past life, fragments of myth" (Brooker 120). These fragments are used by the author as they exist in the author's time, even if they are not truly historical and have been changed over time. This is why mine is not a strictly comparative analysis, but one informed by the popular and intellectual culture of the time. Like Frazer's reference point of the myth of the golden bough in his classic work, or Joyce's reference point to the figure of the hero Ulysses, writers using the mythic method will bring a reference myth to their work, and keep it in the reader's mind throughout the narrative by use of parallel story structure or characters, titles, or fragments of the myth within the text in the form of literary trope, symbolism, or metaphor. In the works of the women studied here, those mythic reference points are seen in implicit and explicit evocations of Demeter and Persephone, Aphrodite, Andromeda, Undine, and Hekate.

It is important to note that in neither the works of these writers, nor the works that Eliot champions, are mythological references substantial and explicit. Brooker explains that for Eliot and his mythical method, "the reference point myth exists as an abstraction. It is not contained in the text, but in the mind of the artist and a reader. Artists do not bring the myth in its entirety; they bring, rather, the information needed to construct the myth" (121). As a result, the myth might exist as a shadow plot or fragmented background myth within the text. Each reader then takes the fragments on the surface of the text and re-collects or re-creates them, thus constructing a variant of the myth and the material of actual life "that will be refined and changed with each reading" (121). As a result, readers become coauthors of the text they are reading in a "mythical method that enables artists and readers to begin with fragments and generate comprehensive abstractions, to begin in isolation and end in community" (121–22). Thus, by looking back through the lens of Eliot's literary theory, it is possible to view the narrative technique of the mythic method in works of late-nineteenth- and early-twentieth-century women writers as both a liberatory and revolutionary process.

Part of the problem I have found in theorizing turn-of-the-twentieth-century women's narratives as revolutionary narratives is the fact that there are relatively few models of women-centered or women-positive theories of identity and subjectivity that can hold Eliot's concepts of complementarity and the complexities of both/and. Thus, I have chosen to use the term "femin(ine)ist" in the course of this analysis because I do not find current philosophical definitions of "woman," "female," "feminine," or "feminist" to be satisfactory individual key terms for a discussion of the complexities of these writers. In short, because these terms participate in the paradox of words discussed below, and while a number of feminist theorists have gone to a great deal of trouble to reclaim and redefine these terms, I still feel that they are rigid and dichotomous terms, dependent on man/male/masculine as their counterparts. Since the writing of the women studied here was nothing if not an attempt to break out of rigid patriarchal dichotomies, I do not consider it appropriate for me to always use male-dependent terminology to describe it.[3] For instance, a quick review of feminist theory reveals that the problem with the use of the term "woman" is that it is drawn from the term "man," and as Simone de Beauvoir explains, woman "is defined and differentiated with reference to man and not he with reference to her; she is the incidental, the inessential as opposed to the essential. He is the Subject, he is the Absolute—she is the Other" (xix).

But this position of Other can also be liberating; thus Luce Irigaray theorizes that "Woman" is the "Volume Without Contours," and the "excess of identity." She is that (witch) which "will not yet have taken (a) place" (53; Irigaray's parenthesis). In this sense, women's narratives become the ultimate witchery that takes power from the language of what Irigaray describes as the "everywhere elsewhere" of woman opposed to the "always already" of patriarchy.[4] Weaving Eliot's theories together with those of de Beauvoir and Irigaray, then, we learn that *woman* is both nothing and everything, the singular and the general, the both/and. She is the everywhere elsewhere, unable to be identified by our current terms except through patriarchal definition. This inability to define and theorize woman as *subject* within modernism reflects the complex dynamics of feminists studying women's writing, as the terms "female," "feminist," and "feminine" all are trapped within a patriarchal definitive reality. As Toril Moi explains, these terms, like the term "woman," are locked within androcentric definitions: "[It is possible to] define as *female*, writing by women, bearing in mind that this label does not say anything at all about the nature of that writing; as *feminist*, writing which takes a discernible anti-patriarchal and anti-sexist position; and as *feminine*, writing which seems to be marginalized (repressed, silenced) by the ruling social/linguistic order. The latter does not (*pace* Kristeva) entail any specific *political* position (no clear-cut feminism), although it does not exclude it either" (132; Moi's emphasis). While these individual categories are useful, they do not help the student of women's narratives theorize their transformative powers that stand at once within the reality of patriarchy where they have been defined by androcentrism, while also existing as the everywhere elsewhere outside of that definition. Thus, I choose to collapse the terms "feminist" and "feminine" together into *femin(ine)ist* in order to better understand women's narratives as those that: 1) develop a textual space that exists in the space between a free woman's reality and the tyranny of patriarchy, and 2) use feminine ambivalence to speak to an imagined framework for feminist alternatives, expressed through narrative.

This femin(ine)ist narrative style reinterprets what Sandra Kemp describes as women's literary strategies of "ellipsis, erasure, obliquity, compression, symbolism, ambiguity [and] the desire to reinvent identity" (100). Thus, patriarchal narrative tools are taken over by women writers to structure a kind of textual "woman's house." In other words, the femin(ine)ist writer uses the narrative strategies of the mythical method to construct her narrative by using the master's tools to dismantle the master's house (to mis-borrow a phrase from Audre Lorde)[5] and to use the resulting debris for the (re)construction of her own. Her narrative shows patriarchy as existing in eternal fear of what it sees as the vacuum of woman's words, of the "not yet," and of the paradox of her ability to exist everywhere elsewhere. She uncovers her narrative little by little and touches upon that which patriarchy seeks to keep hidden: the presence of the everywhere elsewhere of women's experiences.

Stated another way, the femin(ine)ist writer uses language to mediate the conflict between woman and patriarchy. So here she is left with a thesis: patriarchy; and its antithesis: woman; bound up in the synthesis "literature," itself a mediation between patriarchal and femin(ine)ist narrative. Her narrative, then, plays upon this slippage and rides the lines of patriarchal production of meaning through her spiraling construction of literary reality—a powerful, dangerous, and liberatory endeavor. The femin(ine)ist writer recognizes the Word as Arachne's thread that reweaves the power of patriarchy into a web of her own. Thus, the recognition and re-visioning of these strategies of "word-web-warfare" is crucial to this femin(ine)ist analysis.

My study examines the intricacies seen in the intersections along a web of late-nineteenth- and early-twentieth-century women's writing and the relationships between classical figures and liberatory tropes. It represents one way of considering American women writers collected around American modernism that I parallel with a life cycle of femin(ine)ist narrative. The selection of authors I have made here certainly cannot be considered definitive or comprehensive; instead, I have chosen what I consider to be key texts that are representative of the stopping points of what I consider femin(ine)ist modernism. Central to my consideration of this point is their intersection with and use of occult strategies and tropes from classical Greek myth, specifically the authors' use of classical goddess imagery as a way to relocate themselves culturally and to structure a woman-centered vision. Moreover, I argue that the very process of reclaiming and rewriting the stories of classical figures functions as an oblique political commentary that challenges the notion that turn-of-the-twentieth-century women's fiction is generally divorced from overt political concerns—especially in so-called domestic fiction.

Chapter 2 focuses my survey of the theoretical, social, and historical territory that influences the writers studied here. It examines the relationship between classical myth and popular American culture and how the fusion of the two can be seen as forming the foundation for a rich treasure trove of literary symbols. Similarly, this chapter expands my discussion of the literary aspects of myth into a discussion of late-nineteenth- and early-twentieth-century writers' fascination with spirituality and other occult theories. Here, and throughout this study, I will use the term "occult" to signify the secret or extrarational knowledge gained by writers after significant spiritual and philosophical struggle. By tracing mythic and occult themes in the prevailing American culture, I hope to elucidate what I see as a cycle of femin(ine)ist literature that generally moves from a utopian late-nineteenth-century spiritualism to a more dystopian twentieth-century occult modernism.

In chapter 3, I move to a specific analysis of how this group of women authors reconstructs myths that reflect and attempt to resolve the conflicts facing women during specific historic periods. I begin in the time period that frames the cycle of femin(ine)ist modernism in the utopian spiritual narratives of Sarah Orne Jewett's *The Country of the Pointed Firs* (1896) and Emma D. Kelley-Hawkins's *Four Girls at Cottage City* (1898). Using the framework of the myth of Demeter and Persephone, these two novels represent the hope and promise of a new era, one that was influenced by a utopian spiritualism that first called into question the convictions of masculine culture and set the stage for a full realization of femin(ine)ist modernism. These were the women who attempted to create positive women-centered communities with which to mediate the trials and tribulations of patriarchal reality; however, their narratives also investigate the separation of feminist foremothers from their turn-of-the-twentieth-century daughters.

In chapter 4, I contemplate a quartet of narratives woven by the second generation of writers studied here including Onoto Watanna's *Miss Nume of Japan* (1899), Alice Dunbar-Nelson's *A Modern Undine* (c. 1900), and Edith Wharton's *The House of Mirth* (1905) and *The Custom of the Country* (1913). These are narratives that trace the evolution of the goddess Aphrodite as a femin(ine)ist model to her usurped form as the water sprite Undine. This is the period on which the bridge from a feminine utopian mediation of patriarchy to a feminist dystopia rests. Finally, following the turn of the femin(ine)ist cycle, in chapter 5, I will consider one text situated in what I believe to be the "full flowering" of femin(ine)ist modernism in the time period after World War I. Thus, I will examine a Hekatean worldview found in Djuna Barnes's *Nightwood* (1936).

# 2

# Occulted Words and Mythic Worlds

* Keeping in mind the verities of gender, race, class, politics, and philosophies of modernism, what kinds of questions can be asked, what kinds of delineations can be made toward an understanding of late-nineteenth- and early-twentieth-century modernist literature by women? The stereotype sets up this view: she is white, monied enough to expatriate herself to Paris, chooses writing as her vocation only for the sake of the beauty of language itself, while she lives the single exotic life of the exiled intellectual surrounded by the great (male) minds of Europe and America. Her texts are wild, experimental, and beautiful—like herself, and they come from nowhere to flourish in a springtime of high art, only to fade quickly in the winter casualties of World War II. She remains always the youthful Cinderella whose ball was cut short by the midnight stroke of war. Of all the women modernists, only Natalie Barney could fit this description, and she went to great lengths to portray herself as such. Of the women expatriates, Djuna Barnes and Janet Flanner were both working journalists, Kay Boyle was a wife and mother of five children, and Edith Wharton certainly could not be considered "young and wild." Gertrude Stein experienced a kind of exile within the exiles due to her Jewish heritage, age, and sexuality. Both Nella Larsen and Jessie Fauset spent time in Paris, although they

are not regularly considered part of the "expatriate" community. Moreover, significant contributions to modernism were being written stateside, outside of its social and historical parameters, by writers including Willa Cather, Kate Chopin, Alice Dunbar-Nelson, Sui Sin Far, Susan Glaspell, Katherine Anne Porter, Anzia Yezierska, and Onoto Watanna—women writers often marginalized into "ethnic" or "local color" sections of literary anthologies.

In addition to their use of the mythic method, one key to power for writers such as Sarah Orne Jewett, Emma D. Kelley-Hawkins, Onoto Watanna, Alice Dunbar-Nelson, Edith Wharton, and Djuna Barnes was their exploration of women's silence and the failure of words to break open imposed patriarchal restraints on women's speech. These women writers used words that access and reveal the realities of patriarchal rationality and feminist subjectivity. For example, Julia Kristeva explains that under patriarchy, words are used to privilege the symbolic and the paternal, while the semiotic aspects of language are relegated to an exiled other. In her feminist critique of language entitled *The Revolution of Poetic Language* (1974), Kristeva opposes the symbolic aspects of language, which she views as patriarchal and masculine aspects of dominant discourse, with the "semiotic," which she views as a kind of feminine "other" of language. While the semiotic implies language's opposite, it is not an alternative to conventional discourse; instead, like the mythic method, it is one that operates within and necessarily intertwines with traditional narrative and language and is able to subvert its patriarchal aspects. It is fluid and plural in its pleasurable excess over the precise meanings of the symbolic aspects of language. Like the mythic method, the semiotic throws rational dualisms into confusion, and thus readers of semiotic texts are disrupted, unable to take up one position within the binary oppositions of male/female, black/white, sane/mad, et cetera.

Similar to T. S. Eliot's thrill over the possibilities of the mythic text, Kristeva views the semiotic text as that which is truly revolutionary. Moreover, as a layer of the mythic method found in women's writing, this aspect of Kristeva's work is key to understanding late-nineteenth- and early-twentieth-century writers such as Jewett, Kelley-Hawkins, Watanna, Dunbar-Nelson, Wharton, and Barnes. These writers, I contend, understood the power of the semiotic (albeit not in Kristeva's precise, twentieth-century terms) to forge words with indeterminate meanings: ones that reveal cracks, fissures, and disturbances in the matrix of the language used in dominant discourse. For these writers, words became windows opening onto how language serves patriarchal purposes while also opening onto how language can be used to subvert and disrupt that hegemony. In their own way, then, they are Arachnes of modern language, stitching together fragments of personal and fictional experience into a narrative tapestry that tells the story of a new world.

The fiction of these women seized a contradictory power through the faulty medium of words—one that is catachrestic and deliberately paradoxical, creating a narrative destabilization leading to the production of new and different word combinations, which in turn, lead to the production of new and different knowledges about gender, race, class, ideology, or art. This is the "synchronicity of the word" and the "pure linguistic energy" that underlies high modernist style, described by Malcolm Bradbury and James McFarlane (50). Unfortunately for the woman modernist, however, her radical experimentation with narrative forms revealed that words only partially communicate and that they are a paradox because they both mean and fail to mean simultaneously.

Certainly, this is a dimension of modernism that exists in the works of both women and men modernist writers; however, the paradox of words is especially apparent in the works of femin(ine)ist writers. For the writers of the first generation of modernist women writers such as Jewett and Kelley-Hawkins, the power of words was liberating, allowing for transcendent and positive narrations, but writers of subsequent generations such as Onoto Watanna, Edith Wharton, Alice Dunbar-Nelson, and especially Djuna Barnes saw that there is nothing in the words themselves that has any meaning. Because of this, the narratives that characterized the "full flowering" of femin(ine)ist modernism were an attempt to form words into sentences that connote, denote, and emote the semiotic. One result is the triumph of "silence" over the spoken word in Wharton's *The House of Mirth*, as well as Gertrude Stein's evocation of the semiotic in her rhetorical constructions ("a rose is a rose is a rose") or Barnes's complicated and poetic metaphors in *Nightwood*.

In spite of the artistic innovations of these women, they faced cultural difficulties in addition to patriarchal misrecognition of their use of the word, thereupon limiting both the scope and quality of their publications. In a world where most literary endeavors were piloted by white upper-class men, women—and especially women of color—faced an uphill battle to establish careers as artists of letters. In this male-defined world, women often existed in a literal "no man's land" between their mothers' world and that which they imagined for daughters not yet born. As they professionalized themselves as artists for a new century, these women wanted to leave behind the didacticism of abolition and suffrage to look toward a future that could barely be imagined. But too often, androcentric ignorance of these women writers' innovative use of the word meant that their work underwent substantial revision to make it "acceptable" to the male-directed literary market—as in the case of Djuna Barnes's heavily edited *Nightwood*—or it was left rejected and unpublished,[1] as in the case of Alice Dunbar-Nelson's novels. Thus, these women learned early that the occulted or "hidden" narrative was key to staying true to the types of stories that they needed to write.

Above all else, women's modernism was shaped by a radical challenge to linguistic, spiritual, and social conventions, particularly as these writers journeyed further and further from the world of their foremothers into territory marked off as forbidden by patriarchal ideology. For these writers, a reinvention of social and spiritual truths through the alchemy of language was their primary task. In June 1929, the writers who contributed to the full flowering of modernism published the "Proclamation on the Revolution of the Word" in *transition* [*sic*] magazine that expressed twelve foundations of the "New Text." This proclamation was important in its solid definition of the processes of occulted modernist literary technique, as it was a declaration that located the key to new subjective and individual knowledges in the transformative and mystical power of words—a mythical method, I argue, that had been shaped and used by early women modernists such as Sarah Orne Jewett. Their twelve points are:

1. The revolution in the English language is an accomplished fact.
2. The imagination in search of a fabulous world is autonomous and unconfined.
3. Pure poetry is a lyrical absolute that seeks an a priori reality within ourselves alone.
4. Narrative is not mere anecdote, but the projection of a metamorphosis of reality.
5. The expression of these concepts can be achieved only through the rhythmic "Hallucination of the Word."
6. The literary creator has the right to disintegrate the primal matter of words imposed on him by text-books and dictionaries.
7. He has the right to use words of his own fashioning and to disregard existing grammatical and syntactical laws.
8. The "Litany of Words" is admitted as an independent unit.

9. We are not concerned with the propagation of sociological ideas, except to emancipate the creative elements from the present ideology.
10. Time is a tyranny to be abolished.
11. The writer expresses. He does not communicate.
12. The Plain Reader Be Damned. (Fitch 19)

Signed by a collection of progressive writers that included Kay Boyle and Caresse Crosby, the "Proclamation" was the culmination of a literary ideology outlined two years earlier in *transition*'s editorial entitled "Suggestions for a New Magic." Here, the authors rejected "all artistic efforts that fail to subvert the existing concepts of beauty" stating forcefully, "we prefer to skyscraper, spirituality, [and] the immense lyricism and madness of illogic" (Fitch 23). For these writers, narrative was magic—the culmination of an artistic alchemy used to apprehend an unintelligible world.[2] As Howard Fraser explains in his study *In the Presence of Mystery: Modernist Fiction and the Occult*, the transformative power of the alchemy of words was central to modernist literary ideology. Fraser quotes from Cathy Jrade to illustrate his point, writing that "The mythical function of Modernism receives credit as 'the ideological answer to the spirit of crisis.... Since the standard answers no longer appeared viable, Modernist writers sought solutions in unorthodox beliefs and belief systems.... Through the magical powers of language they hoped to break the set patterns of perception, to see beyond disordered appearances, and to capture the perfect harmony of creation'" (quoted in Fraser 24). More important, these tenets of modernism infused the mystical (in a rejection of the rational) with the mythical (in a reinvention of classical ideologies and narratives) to create a semiotic narrative that investigates the speculative, extrarational, and occulted knowledges of modernity.

Positioning themselves as heirs to an occult tradition in literature, these writers strove for the apprehension of what Leon Surette terms a "metaphysical speculation—speculation about the nature of ultimate reality and of our relations to it" (13) within their artistic production. As Surette observes in *The Birth of Modernism*, modernist writers viewed the occult in the early twentieth century as the heir of ancient wisdom, passed on or rediscovered by each new artistic generation in a kind of mystical illumination or communication with the extrarational (known traditionally as the "muse"). Because its adherents were bookish by nature, modernist occultism focused on the point of contact between the human and the sublime (be it good, bad, or indifferent) as gleaned from a tradition of texts including Homer, Ovid, Sappho, Plato, Dante, Blake, Shelley, and Balzac.

By definition, occultists followed their own bent, harvesting usable fragments from major philosophies, ideologies, and spiritualities of the world, yet remaining individualized and distinct from them. If they shared a constant, it was in their abhorrence of all things institutionalized; their choice was instead to privilege myth as a formal and stylistic resource or inspiration. Closely related to this was a view of history that sought to return to the classic Greek text in order to "establish a line of transmission of the gnosis from high antiquity, through the classical and medieval worlds, to the present" (Surette 19). Rejecting the traditional form and content of narrative, poetry, and expression, except that which was found in the ancients, these modernists chose to be truly "radical" (or "to the root"), embracing ancient texts as the origin of pure meaning. For these writers, there was an inherent magic in artistic production, underlined by a spiritual essence (positive, negative, or ambivalent) that provided the energy for what Fraser describes as "the creation of something eternal" (27).

Ironically, the "ancient" literary tradition from which the "anti-institutional" modernists drew inspiration was not so ancient, neither was it anti-institutional, as they tapped into ideologies already present in the late-nineteenth- and early-twentieth-century American cultural milieu.[3] America's fascination with classical Greece was also reinforced by popular images seen in nineteenth-century popular culture and history painting that reflected "a nostalgia for a long-lost Arcadian world untroubled by industry, poverty, ugliness, and the threat of constant change" (Rosenblum and Janson 271). While the influence of classicists such as Jacques-Louis David, Thomas Couture, Alexandre Cabanel, and Adolphe-William Bouguereau on fin-de-siècle writers has begun to be explored by historians of art and literature,[4] certainly the influence on modernist writers of avant-garde artists such as Dante Gabriel Rossetti, Gustave Moreau, Pierre Puvis de Chavannes, Odilon Redon, and Aubrey Beardsley, who also reworked mythological tropes, cannot be underestimated. Certainly, Greek mythology provided a perfect vehicle for an exploration of American cultural upheavals of the late nineteenth and early twentieth century by all variety of artists.

As Jasper Griffin has explained in his analysis of the American fascination with Greek myth in this period of literature, myth is a kind of common property that is "easy to illustrate but difficult to define" (13). Furthermore, the advantage of using mythical stories is in their vague familiarity that is reinforced by their status as "stories of guaranteed importance" (17). The ubiquity and vagueness of classical allusion provided these writers with material that was "ancient," believed to be unspoiled by contemporary prejudices, and "new," as writers creatively rewrote classical stories to suit their own purposes. Greek myth was particularly attractive to American writers at this time, as its celebration of both the sensuous and the intellectual provided a counterpoint to what these writers believed were stringent puritanical Christian ideologies in American culture.[5] Thus, the use of classical Greek myths provided a paradigm for an analysis of American morality and action in fiction.

These aspects of the occult and mythology were important tropes in a tradition of women's modernism that forged together a deeply subversive interest in the unseen and the extrarational with a long-present fascination with classical mythology and ethnic folktales in American popular culture. One can find this reflected, for instance, in allusions to myths of Demeter and Persephone in the fiction of Sarah Orne Jewett and Edith Wharton; the translation of and allusions to Sappho and the ancients in the poetry of Edna St. Vincent Millay, Natalie Barney, and H.D.; the interpretation of Asian myth in the fiction of Sui Sin Far and her sister Onoto Watanna; and the use of Catholic Creole myths in the fiction of Alice Dunbar-Nelson.[6] Moreover, while women writers of color such as Sui Sin Far and Alice Dunbar-Nelson were to an extent able to access mythologies related to their ethnic heritage, without the widespread formal dissemination of these myths, women of color, like their white sisters, looked to classical myth for inspiration. Surette explains that writers of this time period often share a fascination with myth, history, and philosophical and theological thought, and that "It is no small task to attempt to disentangle all of these threads, but it is one that must be undertaken if we are to have a better understanding of the phenomenon of literary modernism" (23). Thus, occult notions that underlie the works of these writers are a vital aspect of my study of women's modernism, and I maintain that the influence of occult knowledges and traditions on modernist women authors cannot be underestimated.

For example, Sarah Orne Jewett maintained an interest in spiritualism after being introduced to the mystical theory of a utopian spiritual world by Professor Theophilus Parsons (Sherman 58), while Alice Dunbar-Nelson was raised by a mother who believed in the "black arts" and "passed along to her daughter a sense of the spiritual and mystical aspects of existence" in the superstitious milieu of late-nineteenth-century New Orleans, which was itself a community that liberally blended elements of Obeah with Catholicism (Hull, *Color* 51). Edith Wharton described her "intense Celtic sense of the super-natural" (Wolff 292), which caused her first to fear, and later to embrace, narratives of ghosts and supernatural events. Djuna Barnes grew up in a household frequented by "occult happenings," as her grandmother Zadel was an accomplished medium who channeled spirits that included Franz Liszt and Jack London (Herring 44). Although she is not part of this study of American writers, one of the most documented associations between the occult and a (British) modernist woman writer is Radclyffe Hall's conversion to spiritualism after pursuing an investigation into the presence of her dead lover Ladye with her then lover Una Troubridge. Hall referred to the triad as "our three selves" and used this phrase as the dedication to many of her novels (Baker 3). She and Troubridge were also important members of the Society for Psychical Research, an organization founded to investigate the scientific nature of occult happenings (3).

An attraction to the occult by these writers was not seen as peculiar in the time period spanning the mid-nineteenth century to the early part of the twentieth. As Ann Braude writes in *Radical Spirits,* the rise of spiritualism paralleled that of the women's rights movement after its inception in 1848, and "the two movements intertwined continually as they spread throughout the country" (2). These first utopian manifestations of occult practices in America appealed to the progressive ideals of the generation born around the time of the Civil War. As Braude explains, one of the foundational principles of spiritualism was its emphasis on the individual's own notion of truth and a greater good, an emphasis that empowered women: "Such individualism laid the foundation for spiritualism's rejection of male headship over women—or indeed of any individual over any other—whether in religion, politics, or society. Spiritualists believed that the advent of spirit communication heralded the arrival of a new era, one in which humanity, with spirit guidance, would achieve hitherto impossible levels of development. The new era would be characterized by the accomplishment of a broad program of progressive social reforms and a complete reformation of personal life" (6). While offering women an opportunity to exercise leadership and religious authority, early occult philosophies within spiritualism emphasized a classical social order where gender equality would reign supreme. As a utopian worldview that promised comfort, Howard Kerr writes, late-nineteenth-century spiritualism was a beneficial "phenomenal proof of a life to come" that gave grieving postwar friends and relatives great consolation through communication with their dead (108). In addition, many believed "that spiritualism could mediate between faith and science by providing empirically verifiable evidence of immortality," thus reassuring survivors that their loved ones were spending eternity in a pleasant, heavenly state (109).

In its effort to capture and explain human nature, the rise of spiritualism in America also saw the ascending popularity of religious-scientific philosophies such as Swedenborgianism, Mary Baker Eddy's theories of Christian Science, and the powerful and popular triad of mesmerism, clairvoyance, and phrenology. Ultimately, the spiritual nature of these philosophies gave way to more "scientific" theories such as Sigmund Freud's psychoanalysis. An interest in Eastern religious cosmologies and the occult also developed at this time, "especially [in] those who longed for radical social and political change" (Washington 25). One of the most notorious gurus of the time was Madame Blavatsky and her Theosophical Society, who represented the idealistic tenets of the turn of the twentieth century in their advocacy of a universal human brotherhood without regard to race, creed, or gender; encouraged comparative studies between the religious, philosophical, and scientific; and investigated unexplained laws of nature and latent human powers (69). Another notorious guru was the Russian mystic and dancemaster George Ivanovitch Gurdjieff who turned from the idealistic tenets of Theosophy to a philosophy of "barbarism and primitivism" (170) that highlighted the ideology of man as the noble savage and encouraged its students to become conscious of their true selves and to cease being human machines. For Gurdjieff, this practice could not be a pleasant one, and the process was "enhanced" with an emphasis on stress, pain, tension, and conflict. Gurdjieff's philosophy is one that is linked explicitly by Peter Washington in *Madame Blavatsky's Baboon* to the Left Bank lesbian expatriate circle that included Jane Heap, Margaret Anderson, Djuna Barnes, and Janet Flanner (288). Gurdjieff's ideals also surface in Harlem, with Thadious Davis linking a study group led by Gurdjieff disciple Jean Toomer to writers including Nella Larsen (167).

The attraction to Gurdjieff's nihilistic philosophies by the "lost" generation of modernists becomes understandable when it is put into relief by the forward-looking and optimistic ideologies of an earlier generation of writers that included Jewett and Kelley-Hawkins. Here it is possible to identify a modernist cycle that moves from a utopian spiritual ideology (often aligned with classical or Christian ideals) to a period of crisis that ultimately results in a dystopian and nihilistic spiritual death in the "full flowering" of high modernist ideals. But like any other ideological movement, spiritualism changed over time as it responded to historical and social events. Thus, it is important to note the transformation from a more positive and utopian spiritualism practiced in the latter part of the nineteenth century to a more nihilistic and dystopian, or occult spiritualism in the years after World War I.

This change is not surprising when readers understand that, stripped of its idealized canonical posturing, the modern age cannot be considered "glorious" as it is in so many literary and historical studies. For the women of early modernism, the horrors of the American Civil War were still in America's collective memory, when even more unimaginable horrors of the early twentieth century's pestilences of disease, economic depressions, and war were heaped upon drastic changes in science and technology.[7] These revolutions turned the known world upside down for the writers of the lost generation, and for them, modernism became morbidity in an endless cycle of empty promises and economic struggles in an age that was supposed to be marvelous and new.

Djuna Barnes summed up the attitude of her generation in her answer to the question "Why such morbidity?" posed by Guido Bruno in an interview for *Pearson's Magazine* in 1919:

> "Morbid?" was her cynical answer. "You make me laugh. This life I write and draw and portray is life as it is, and therefore you call it morbid. Look at my life. Look at the life around me. Where is this beauty that I am supposed to miss? The nice episodes that others depict? Is not everything morbid? I mean the life of people stripped of their masks. Where are the relieving features?
>
> "Often I sit down to work at my drawing board, at my typewriter. All of a sudden my joy is gone. I feel tired of it all because, I think, 'What's the use?' Today we are, tomorrow dead. We are born and don't know why. We live and suffer and strive, envious or envied. We love, we hate, we work, we admire, we despise. . . . Why? And we die, and no one will ever know that we have been born." (Barry 386)

Speaking for her generation of lost women, Barnes outlines the attitude of many women writers at what will be the final turn of the femin(ine)ist modernist cycle.

# 3

## Unraveling Demeter's Garden

*Demeter and Persephone in the Works of Sarah Orne Jewett and Emma D. Kelley-Hawkins*

\*  Sarah Orne Jewett (b. 1849) and Emma D. Kelley-Hawkins (n.d.) are members of the first generation of women examined in this study. The women of this generation were born during the crisis times leading up to the Civil War and came of age during America's Great Awakening in the cultural tumult of the Civil War and Reconstruction. This generation included women writers and activists such as Harriet Tubman, Frances E. W. Harper, Victoria Woodhull, Elizabeth Stuart Phelps Ward, Anna Green, Carry Nation, Mary Foote, Alice James, Emma Lazurus, Ella Wheeler Wilcox, Mary E. Wilkins Freeman, Pauline Hopkins, and Charolotte Perkins Gilman. These women were members of a progressive group that urged racial tolerance, fought for the Fifteenth Amendment, and debated the practicalities of Social Darwinism. Overwhelmed by the crises of war and depressions, they looked forward to an idealistic American future celebrated in the 1876 American Centennial Exhibition in Philadelphia and witnessed the monopolization of awards for American products at the Paris World's Fair in 1878. This was the generation that struggled to lay the groundwork for a new, peaceful order that was predicted to come in the new twentieth century.

Sarah Orne Jewett's *The Country of the Pointed Firs* (1896) and

Emma D. Kelley-Hawkins's *Four Girls at Cottage City* (1898) begin this literary cycle with the hope and promise of a new era of femin(ine)ist subjectivity as they explore the realities and hopeful possibilities of women who attempt to mediate the hardships of a patriarchal world. Theirs was a logical strategy for women immersed in popular late-nineteenth-century notions of spiritualism and Christianity that foresaw a utopian and egalitarian future guided by women. Sarah Orne Jewett, as Elizabeth Ammons explains, was especially representative of the popular late-nineteenth-century spiritualist cultural movement: "In particular she seems to have believed that there existed a type of therapeutic female psychic energy which could be communicated telepathically and which could operate both to bond individuals and to create a spiritual community—or occult sisterhood—among women in general" (Ammons, "Jewett's Witches" 168). Certainly, middle-class white women like Sarah Orne Jewett cautiously relished the social changes of the late nineteenth century for the freedom and autonomy they offered. These might have included independent living in an apartment away from large family households, ready-to-wear clothing bought from department stores that freed them from the drudgery of daily sewing, and new occupations that allowed economic freedom from the certain fate of marriage. Yet these women also took seriously what Marianne DeKoven describes as the "potential for bringing on retribution from a still-empowered patriarchy" ("Gendered Doubleness" 21) in the form of exploitative wage scales, limited career advancement, and certain sexual harassment for the unchaperoned or unaccompanied. Similarly, middle-class black women like Emma D. Kelley-Hawkins surveyed the violent and racist social territory of late-nineteenth-century America with a cautiously sharp eye. As such, the fictions of Jewett and Kelley-Hawkins carefully look to the utopian gaps that existed between an imagined freedom and the realities of the isolation of women under patriarchy's sexism and black women under its violent racism.

The paradoxes of living within and wanting to live without a racist patriarchy, as well as the tensions between the precarious natures of being a woman or person of color under its regime, created a powerful ambivalence in the works of femin(ine)ist writers such as Jewett and Kelley-Hawkins who wished to create safe spaces for women in fiction. As Sandra Gilbert and Susan Gubar explain, these pressures on late-nineteenth-century women authors produced texts that often seem "odd" when compared to the traditional white male literary paradigm; however, a deviation from traditional literary styles allowed these women to write texts "that are in some sense palimpsestic, works whose surface designs conceal or obscure deeper, less accessible (and less socially acceptable) levels of meaning" (*Madwoman* 73). Thus, women like Jewett and Kelley-Hawkins tell their femin(ine)ist stories by "following Emily Dickinson's famous (and characteristically female) advice to 'Tell all the Truth but tell it slant—'" (73).

Similarly, Karen Kaivola explains that outright challenges to the racist and sexist patriarchy "would have been too risky" for late-nineteenth-century women writers (2); so instead, they were forced to resort to resisting patriarchy through a web of contradictory forms embedded in their texts. As a result, the liberatory truths of *Four Girls at Cottage City* and *The Country of the Pointed Firs* must be teased out from under a surface meaning that obscures the unsayable under patriarchy yet simultaneously articulates revolutionary femin(ine)ist positions. Hence, the reader must unlock the shared secret discourse of these texts to unbraid meanings, a textual code as it were, embedded in the narratives. Readers must approach femin(ine)ist texts in this way, as it was necessary for writers like Jewett and Kelley-Hawkins to obscure the femin(ine)ist messages and meanings of their texts, to "record their own dreams and their own stories *in disguise*," to complete their projects and circumvent patriarchal retribution (Gilbert and Gubar, *Madwoman* 73).

It is in the works of these women that the beginnings of a femin(ine)ist occult hermeneutics can be seen, as their decision to write about isolation "involves risk and ambivalence" compelling them to create textual subjects that are simultaneously revealed and concealed (Kaivola 2). The use of this narrative technique suggests that transgressions of patriarchy "as seen and experienced from female perspectives must remain disguised, hidden and displaced" (3). As the use of this literary strategy is understood, then, the texts of late-nineteenth-century women writers do not seem so naive, far-fetched, or oblique. They are narratives that focus on occulted, displaced, or disguised expressions of revolt, creating powerful, subversive commentaries on women's experiences under patriarchy. Moreover, they are texts written by women who came of age during an American economic and social high in the first blush of the promises of social equality, so they embrace modern, progressive, and utopian possibilities for women-centered communities existing outside the bounds of patriarchal rule.

Accordingly, these texts often present themselves as an odd mixture of the positive and the negative, the obvious and the obscure. Stated another way, their texts exist at the sanguine beginning of the femin(ine)ist modernist cycle, where the realities of hardships suffered by women under the tyranny of patriarchy are converted to positive tales of women's community in *The Country of the Pointed Firs*—or of a girls' community in *Four Girls at Cottage City*.[1] Women writers such as Sarah Orne Jewett attempted to create subjective women-centered communities with which to temper the trials and tribulations of patriarchal reality through what can be termed the "magical safety" of women's words. Although their challenge to patriarchy was by no means "safe" for their careers as literary artists, their worlds of words strove to create a subjective artistic temporality of another time and place that was a fictional "safe space" for readers. This "magical safety" exists in the gap between patriarchal reality and total femin(ine)ist subjectivity and is fully developed in *The Country of the Pointed Firs* as an example of women's reality that exists both within yet without patriarchy. Because it exists at this midpoint, Jennifer Bailey explains that it has been easy to miss the importance of Jewett's project (285). For Bailey, masculinist readings focus on Jewett's text as simply a version of plotless "local color" fiction, but "a female reading [. . .] discovers a world that uses setting symbolically in order to portray a female version of nature and the nature of the female" (285). Within Bailey's framework, then, reading Jewett's text as a playful femin(ine)ist "misuse" of proscribed narrative traditions opens a variety of subversive possibilities.

Jewett's literary strategies produce a powerful narrative that weaves together the interaction of female authors and readers, feminine texts, and feminist ideals into what Sandra Kemp considers a new "gender-genre-modernism" that "offers possibilities for new female subject positions through the creation of a new kind of temporality" (100). This is exactly the effect of *Pointed Firs* and *Four Girls* when femin(ine)ist space is carved out of a world dominated by men through the power of women's words. This distinct mode of textual production abolishes distinctions between internal and external worlds, collapsing the narrative into a femin(ine)ist prose where text, meaning, and metaphor merge to create a truly deconstructive text. Readers must exist in a circular reality with the text in the "space that exists outside plot" where *meaning*, in the traditional sense, cannot be ferreted out of hierarchical layers of text (104); hence, a femin(ine)ist reading of these narratives participates in the authors' exploration and reconstruction of the disowned and disavowed (by patriarchy) realm of femin(ine)ist subjectivity.

This technique is an important strategy for understanding *The Country of the Pointed Firs,* Jewett herself explained, as she was well aware of the reader's role in the text when she termed it "imaginative realism," saying: "A story should be managed so that it should *suggest* interesting things to the *reader* instead of the author's doing all the thinking for him, and setting it before him in black and white" (quoted in Donovan, "Jewett's Critical Theory" 216; Jewett's emphasis). (It is interesting that Jewett's use of the male pronoun here seems to direct her comments specifically at the male reader who might find himself outside of the "code" of feminine prose.) Josephine Donovan illuminates Jewett's comment when she asserts that the reader has an active role in her texts, weaving together the reader's lived experiences with those of the literary characters to create a new subjective reality. Donovan explains that Jewett "extended her conception of authorial restraint to the point where she allowed the reader a creative role in the process. The author should not attempt to exert complete control over the reader's thoughts, but rather attempt to communicate images that 'open seed' in the reader's mind, that allow the reader to intuit meanings beyond the literal" (217). The shared experience of author-text-reader is itself a kind of literary magic, establishing a place of refuge for the reader in the utopian temporality of Jewett's closed women's world.

So where, then, does a specifically femin(ine)ist reading of *Pointed Firs* begin?

It begins with a consideration of Jewett's narrative tropes drawn from the myth of Demeter and Persephone. As readers may recall, this myth is a powerful story of the bond between mother and daughter broken by men. While innocently picking flowers out of sight of her mother, Persephone is abducted and raped by Hades. Alerted by the screams of her daughter, Demeter is unable to immediately intervene and rescue her; thus, she puts on clothes of mourning, lights a torch, and begins the search for her lost daughter. Shortly into her search, Demeter meets up with Hekate, who leads her to Helios, himself a witness to Persephone's abduction. Helios reports that by Zeus's permission, Hades has stolen Persephone and made her his wife—a marriage that cannot be dissolved. Upon hearing this, Demeter's mourning grows deeper, and she takes her revenge by causing all the fields of the Earth to become unfruitful, endangering both its inhabitants and the gods of Olympus who depend on Earthly sacrifices. Demeter's wrath captures the attention of Zeus, who sends Hermes to return Persephone to her mother. Hades consents, but only after tricking Persephone into eating a tiny pomegranate seed.

Although she returns to her mother, Persephone is commanded to spend one third of the year in Hades's underworld as a result of eating the seed.

As Donovan demonstrates, this mother-daughter myth was particularly attractive to late-nineteenth-century women writers: "The Demeter-Persephone myth is singularly relevant to the historical transition that occurred in middle-class women's culture in the late nineteenth century in the Western world. It allegorizes the transformation from a matricentric preindustrial culture—Demeter's realm—to a male-dominated capitalist-industrialist ethos, characterized by growing professionalism and bureaucracy: the realm of patriarchal captivity" (*After the Fall* 2).[2] If Demeter stands as an allegory for the idealized world of pre-industrial America, theorizes Donovan, "Persephone represents the daughters who leave the sphere of the mothers and enter a period of patriarchal captivity" (3). But beyond these surface allegories of the cultural and social upheaval in women's lives at this time, the Demeter-Persephone myth also operates as a vehicle for expressing the painful loss of femin(ine)ist subjectivity—and the attempt to reclaim it. As Gail Thomas explains, "It is more than the loss of a child by the mother, more than a loss of the feminine; it is a lament for the loss of the deep spiritual realms that are reached through an unbroken feminine essence" (38). Or, as Elizabeth T. Hayes explains, the myth of Persephone symbolizes the experience of women under patriarchy: "The myth [...] valorizes female ways of being and acting. It explores Demeter and Persephone's response to patriarchal law and power, highlighting the women's valuing of relationship, of unity, of conjunction over the separation and hierarchical ordering valued by the male gods" (4). Hence, the story of Demeter and Persephone reaches deep beyond the mother's lament to "the passionate desire to be connected with a realm which has been disowned and disavowed" (Thomas 45).

In Sarah Way Sherman's terms, Jewett's novel "gave this myth new life" (x). Seen in this context, Jewett's novel can be placed at the apex of the femin(ine)ist modernist cycle to stand, like Demeter, as a kind of mother figure against which later authors can rebel or, alternatively, valorize. Jewett's fictional characters embody the spirit of the "Great Mother" and exist in a matrifocal community of Dunnet Landing that espouses many of the core themes of the Great Mother's society: freedom for women, democratic political principles, progressive views, and simple pleasures (Walker, *Encyclopedia* 689). In Jewett's novel, most of Dunnet Landing's men have been lost at sea or relocated away from the town due to the whaling era's decline. She invites her readers—or those outside of her world of women—into her text by creating a young, unnamed female narrator, an outsider to Dunnet Landing, with whom readers can identify. This is a community where the daily routines and rhythms of women are primary—knitting, visiting, gardening—as its inhabitants confront issues of living in a woman-centered discontinuity within the patriarchal "underworld."

*The Country of the Pointed Firs* opens with a firm allusion to Persephone in the chapter entitled "The Return," when the young narrator arrives at the Mother's world of Dunnet Landing described as "the centre of civilization of which her affectionate dreams had told" (2) abruptly contrasting the "civilization" of this woman- and mother-centered community with the "uncivilized" world of the patriarchal fathers. Immediately, the reader recognizes that this is not a usual bustling coastal community, as it is represented by the torpid matriarch Mrs. Almira Todd. Ammons explains that "In this dreamy place, she [the narrator] is welcomed by motherly, ample Almira Todd, an herbalist whose last name rhymes with *god* and whose first name brings to mind the Latin word *alma*, soul" (*Conflicting Stories* 47). Moreover, Mrs. Todd is closely linked to her community of "pointed firs" through a firm association of her given name, Almira, with the old Irish name for the fir, *Ailm*, which according to folklorist Steve Blamires, "comes from a [word] root that can mean 'that which goes forward' and also 'will or desire'" (184). Furthermore, the vowel associated with *Ailm* in the ancient tree alphabet is "A" or "aah," which Blamires explains can represent a range of emotions: it "can express both amazement and wonder, as well as the experience of reaching the solution to a problem. At the other end of the scale, it can be a cry or groan indicating physical or mental pain. It is, in a sense, the opposite ends of the range of human endurance or experience" (183).[3] This association is particularly relevant for Jewett's metaphorical structure, as it represents the subjectivity of meaning through inflection.

Like Jewett's text, the symbolic and spiritual aspects of the fir are difficult to grasp, Blamires illustrates, requiring the practitioner to abandon traditional logic in favor of intuition and a spiritual approach to understanding meaning (185). In sharp contrast to the exploitative realities of the late-nineteenth-century working woman's twelve- or fourteen-hour factory workdays for low wages, or the cultural pull to keep her the "angel of the house," supported by a man, raising his children, and keeping his house, Jewett's text represents a woman-centered community carved out of these repressions of patriarchy. In this context, the fir is a particularly useful metaphor for a woman's social position. Barbara Walker explains, "Evergreens in general were powerful symbols of ongoing life or immortality, because they seemed to keep themselves alive when everything else died during the winter" (Walker, *Dictionary* 464). Thus, the symbolic forest setting of *The Country of the Pointed Firs* works well with Jewett's invocation of Demeter, who herself remained steadfast in the face of loss.

Compressed into the character of Mrs. Todd is a powerful connection to the world of Demeter and the mother-goddesses, as Mrs. Todd is "a very large person" who exists outside of the fashionable and corseted young women of patriarchal desire and spends her time gathering and growing "a rustic pharmacopoeia" of herbs and medicinal concoctions to treat her female neighbors (Jewett 3). Her healing powers and motherly interaction with the town's inhabitants show that Mrs. Todd is connected to a spiritual knowledge that ordinary women cannot access. Mrs. Todd may not be a literal "mother," but she exists in the reality of *Mothers* where she takes care of everyone; however, her position as a symbolic Mother leaves her with the ambiguous and painful destiny of mediating between patriarchy and the daughters of Dunnet Landing. As the narrator observes, "An absolute, archaic grief possessed this countrywoman; she seemed like a renewal of some historic soul, with her sorrows and the remoteness of a daily life busied with rustic simplicities and the scents of primeval herbs" (49). Like all earthly mothers, Mrs. Todd negotiates her path with a divided self, knowing that she can open the doors to other existential possibilities for her daughters, yet she is always burdened with the knowledge that she cannot travel through them herself—those paths are for the Persephones of the younger generation to travel.

As a mystical mediator between fragile women and the tribulations of patriarchy, Mrs. Todd is closely aligned with thyme, a magical herb used to increase strength and courage, and, as well, an herb that allows those who use it as an amulet to see past this earthly world into that of the spirits (Dunwich 42, 170). She is "an ardent lover of herbs" whose "queer little garden" is "puzzling to a stranger," or in other words, puzzling to those who are uninitiated in the secrets of Demeter's command of growing things (Jewett 3–4). As a symbolic form of the mother-goddess, Mrs. Todd has the ability to "trod heavily upon thyme" (time), to create a closed world of safety for the women of Dunnet Landing, and she is connected to the "remembrance of something in the forgotten past," to "sacred and mystic rites," and to herbs with "some occult knowledge handed with them down through the centuries" (3–4).

The concluding paragraph of the chapter entitled "Mrs. Todd" sums up her sibylic powers, associating her with what folklorist Barbara Walker describes as one of the "most powerful oracular priestesses" (*Dictionary* 277): "She stood in the center of a braided rug, and its rings of black and gray seemed to circle about her feet in the dim light. Her height and massiveness in the low room gave her the look of a huge sibyl, while the strange fragrance of the mysterious herb blew in from the little garden" (8). Marked by the ability to change reality through her magical use of words and herbs, Mrs. Todd is linked to a powerful matristic mythological language. This use of discourse through the trope of the sibyl is explained by Julia Kristeva in her essay "From Symbol to Sign," where the image of the sibyl exists as a "hybrid, double, ambiguous figure" (67) who introduces a blend of alterity and negativity, along with the natural and the supernatural, into discourse. According to Kristeva, "We might say that the image of the Sibyl is that of the infinitization of discourse, the figuralization of the word as it were liberated from its dependence on the symbol and enjoying the 'arbitrariness' of the sign. Belonging to this and not the other world, the Sibyl speaks all languages, possesses the future, reunites improbable elements both in and through the word. The unlimited possibilities of discourse, which the sign (novel) will try to represent, are symbolized in this transitory figure [of the sibyl]" (68). Mrs. Todd, "a huge sibyl" (Jewett 8), stands enshrined in the circles of the rug, marking her presence as a feminine occult figure. Walker explains that, "The circle was always one of the primary feminine signs [. . .] associated with the idea of a protected or consecrated space, the center of the motherland, a ceremonial space where all participants were equal" (*Dictionary* 4). Thus, the sibyl's symbol of the circle creates a narrative temporality wherein readers achieve meaning within the alchemy of femin(ine)ist safety.

The metaphorical use of Demeter and the sibyl, then, marks Jewett's work with the hallmarks of femin(ine)ist discourse and occult hermeneutics, which is not lost upon the young narrator who also falls under Mrs. Todd's "spell" (7). Mrs. Todd stands in command of this world with her word as her weapon, and as sibyl, she is marked with a positive power to change the negativity of the patriarchal world into a feminine and matriarchal one through her use of femin(ine)ist discourse. It is here that *The Country of the Pointed Firs* reveals the synchronicity of language through the magic of narrative that is fundamental to the mythic method of femin(ine)ist modernism. Without this impetus, the narrative stands only as a collection of unrelated words on the page and images in the mind; with it, the reader is transported to another time and place—indeed, to another subjective reality that transcends the boundaries of patriarchal strictures.

Mrs. Todd is clearly associated with Demeter's symbols of the feminine occult or witchcraft; however, as Elizabeth Ammons notes, she is marked as "guide and healer rather than as destroyer" ("Jewett's Witches" 169). More important, as both sibyl and the "oracle that she was" (Jewett 85) as well as the guide to the "remembrance of something in the forgotten past" (3), Mrs. Todd seemingly answers Ammons's questions: "What are the extraordinary powers available to women who maintain rather than forsake woman's ancient identification with the occult? What, in other words, is the living power of the witch?" ("Jewett's Witches" 168). Indeed, Mrs. Todd demonstrates that the living power of the witch is the ability to carve out a wary temporality for the world's harried female inhabitants.

Like the caves sibyls live in, the "dim light" and the "low room" of Mrs. Todd's house allude to the thresholds of Persephone's underworld (Jewett 8). In Dunnet Landing, the narrator finds herself in this consecrated female space of Mrs. Todd's house, where she is protected from the hardships of patriarchy and granted equality with women in the safety of this femin(ine)ist environment. Significantly, Jewett inverts the traditional structure of Persephone's descent and return, to have her Persephone/narrator first *return* to Dunnet Landing from the city, which can be seen as a metaphorical (patriarchal) underworld in contrast to the woman-centered pastoral world of Dunnet Landing. It is important to note that in the text's play on the myth of Demeter and Persephone, the three main characters of Mrs. Blackett, Mrs. Todd, and the narrator blend to form the three manifestations of the mother-goddess respectively as crone, mother, and virgin. This is reinforced through their connection to the name *Demeter:* in Greek, the second part of the term *mater* is "mother," and the first is *De,* the delta or triangle (Walker, *Encyclopedia* 218). In the metaphorical form of Demeter, Mrs. Todd functions as the eternal Mother, one part of the tripartite version of the Goddess, Mrs. Blackett functions as the crone, while both women are supplemented by the narrator as Persephone, or virgin, because she has not yet been initiated into the secrets of Dunnett Landing's feminine world.

While *Pointed Firs* reveals an occult emphasis on the cyclical and routine nature of women's lives, it decenters the reader's expectations of standard linear narratives when it inverts Persephone's reunion celebration at her return and the funeral at her leave-taking. Instead of beginning with celebration (Springtime in the myth), Mrs. Todd's first substantial social activity of the text is to attend a funeral, thus inverting the traditional structure of the myth of Demeter and Persephone. Jewett rewrites and plays with the myth of Persephone in such a way that the social action of the text begins with what can be read as a symbolic funeral for patriarchy's power within the woman's community of Dunnet Landing in order to bring the narrator into a closed female system mediated within the gaps of patriarchy. But *The Country of the Pointed Firs* reclaims the power of Persephone's isolation by converting her traditional ingestion of the pomegranate seed to that of the narrator's ingestion of Mrs. Todd's camomile [*sic*] beer after the funeral. As the narrator explains, the beer is a secret concoction, guarded deep within Mrs. Todd's sibylline cave and reserved only for initiates:

> I heard her going down into the cool little cellar, and then there was considerable delay. When she returned, mug in hand, I noticed the taste of camomile, in spite of my protest; but its flavor was disguised by some other herb that I did not know, and she stood over me until I drank it all and said that I liked it.
>
> "I don't give that to everybody," said Mrs. Todd kindly; and I felt for a moment as if it were part of a spell and incantation, and as if my enchantress would now begin to look like the cobweb shapes of the arctic town. (30–31)

Because the narrator swallows the beer, her participation in the women's community of Dunnet Landing is ensured for at least a season, just as Persephone's residence in Hades was guaranteed for a season because she ingested the pomegranate seed. It is significant that after this episode the narrator ceases the literary production she began in the schoolhouse. She has been disengaged from her isolation of producing a masculine written word to become a part of Dunnet Landing's female oral community, which is primary to Mrs. Todd's art. The women of the novel ground themselves in an occulted femin(ine)ist oral culture to knit together a shield of narration that protects them from patriarchal intrusion. Their stories and words are for pleasure, not for control or power. Their conversation is always living; therefore, the narrator cannot practice the dead language of words on paper in the environment of living conversation in Dunnet Landing.

Jewett's playful reversal of the traditional mythic structure continues with the narrator's leave-taking at the *end* of the novel where Persephone's disengagement from Demeter's matrifocal domain to "return to the world in which I feared to find myself as stranger" (129) is treated as a characteristically somber moment. But before the Persephone/narrator's departure, her full equality in Demeter's realm is ritualistically celebrated when she is allowed to participate in the Bowden reunion with Mrs. Todd, Mrs. Blackett, and Mrs. Fosdick. At the reunion, however, where she is surrounded by an entire community of Bowden witch women, the narrator initially misreads the simplicity and sanctuary of the Bowden community since her vision continues to be influenced by patriarchal standards: "More than one face among the Bowdens showed that only opportunity and stimulus were lacking,—a narrow set of circumstances had caged a fine able character and held it captive" (107). The "opportunity and stimulus" that the narrator misreads as "lacking" for the witch women of the Bowden clan, such as Mrs. Todd and Mrs. Blackett, is instead the calm character influenced by the safe space organized within patriarchy by the living power of Bowden woman-witchcraft. Because the narrator cannot yet understand this, she must continue to journey through the underworld of the patriarchy/city and back again to Dunnet Landing's women's community in a cycle of femin(ine)ist maturity.

As a precursor to the dystopian tradition of femin(ine)ist modernism, *The Country of the Pointed Firs* hints at the future lives of women that will be explored in the later turn of the femin(ine)ist modernist cycle by writers in the social chaos between the wars. For instance, the narrative of "Poor Joanna" foreshadows life as it will be for expatriated women of the early twentieth century, for Joanna is a woman who has been alienated by life's events and moves to Shell-Heap Island. Mrs. Fosdick explains, "All she wanted was to get away from folks, she thought she wasn't fit to live with anybody, and wanted to be free" (65). Sadly, Joanna cannot bear even the mediated safety of patriarchy that exists in Dunnet Landing, and she finds it necessary to reinvent herself in the isolation of Shell-Heap Island.

Joanna's story begins with hints at a troubled time to come, told on "a chilly night of cold northeasterly rain" (62), hinting at the presence of an "untellable" woman's tale. It is a story that must be spoken under cover of feminine darkness, because it reveals one woman's disengagement from patriarchy. Originally, Joanna expatriated herself to Shell-Heap Island because she was "crossed in love," but as Mrs. Fosdick explains, "I can see that Joanna was one doomed from the first to fall into a melancholy" (65). Joanna's isolated expatriation, however, has subsequently been transformed into a woman-centered existence, as her separation from Dunnet Landing allows her the autonomy to attempt to create a woman's life in what Elaine Showalter terms a "wild zone of women's culture" outside of patriarchy ("Feminist Criticism" 262). For Showalter, this wild zone can be defined in three ways: "Spatially it stands for an area which is literally no-man's-land, a place forbidden to men [. . .]. Experientially it stands for the aspects of the female life-style which are outside of and unlike those of men [. . . and] metaphysically, or in terms of consciousness" (262). Unable to bear the confining mediation of patriarchy that takes place within Dunnet Landing, Joanna's separation grants her freedom to create a woman-centered existence that is free from all aspects of patriarchy, since it takes place outside of its restrictive enclosure.

Significantly, Joanna chooses her life as "a sort of nun or hermit" living "for years all alone" (65) on Shell-Heap Island, which is surrounded by rumors of "savage cannibals" and "Indian captives." The racism of these rumors in the mouths of the characters is not lost on the contemporary reader, nor does it seem to be lost on Jewett, who rebuts the rumors through Mrs. Todd who says, "but I never could believe it. There never was no cannibals on the coast 'o Maine" (63). Forging an alliance between the misunderstood and the outcast, the character of Joanna represents a kind of coming together of marginalized peoples: "an old Chief resided there [who] once ruled the winds" (63). Joanna, in her wild zone, claims the place of this male wind-divinity and takes its power as her own, standing upon the power of one marginalized deity and uniting her feminine power with it as she metaphorically prophesies the future for women.[4] Unable anymore to connect to patriarchal language, Joanna meets visitors Mrs. Todd and the Minister "not sayin' a word" (72) and she "had but little to say" (74) to her visitors. Thus, Joanna voluntarily enters the wild zone that is, as Showalter explains, "the place for the revolutionary women's language" that cannot be understood by those whose understanding is still structured by the dominant discourse (263).

Some residents of Dunnet Landing recognize the power of Joanna's silent expatriation, as more than twenty years after her death, her island "was not without its pilgrims" (Jewett 81). Joanna's gravesite becomes a "shrine of solitude" that allows others to envision their own escape into the wild zone. The narrator explains that Joanna's choice will not be forgotten, as "the feet of the young find them out because of curiosity and dim foreboding; while the old bring hearts full of remembrance" (82). Joanna has fully severed herself from the reality of the Fathers, though she allows some connection with the

Mothers to remain through her relationship with Mrs. Todd; but ultimately, even that connection is severed, as Mrs. Todd cannot give up the safety of her carved-out woman's sphere to commune with a rebellious Joanna in the wild zone, and Joanna must live out her life in isolation.

The power of Joanna's isolation allows her to live a full woman's artistic life of gardening and weaving reeds into mats, cushions, and shoes (74–75); but Joanna, like many women modernists of the later generation of 1914, has "lost her hope" (76) and "cannot brave the sight of men" (82). Joanna tells Mrs. Todd that her self-imposed exile is because she has "committed the unpardonable sin" (76) and must live apart from the other women in order to avoid patriarchal retribution on them for her behavior. Possibly, the "unpardonable sin" would have been understood in Jewett's time as the "sin" of disconnecting one's self from human communion. But interestingly, Jewett's allusion to this Puritan term in the context of Joanna's story creates yet another subversion of patriarchal precepts in making the "sin" a disconnection from women's communion. While readers speculate about the nature of Joanna's "sin," it is also possible that it might be of a sexual nature, as the narrator observes, "There was something mediaeval [sic] in the behavior of poor Joanna Todd under a disappointment of the heart" (69). While the text never provides a clear reference to explain Joanna's transgression, it seems to have had significant repercussions for the women of Dunnet Landing. As Mrs. Fosdick explains, alluding to Joanna as a precursor to the expatriates: "I expect nowadays, if such a thing happened, she'd have gone out West . . . or up to Massachusetts. . . . The World's bigger an' freer than it used to be" (77). Mrs. Todd, however, refuses to believe that Joanna's "sin" is as great as it is made out to be if it is seen through matriarchal eyes instead of patriarchal: "'Tis like bad eyesight, the mind of such a person: if your eyes don't see right there may be a remedy, but there's no kind of glasses to remedy the mind" (77–78). Mrs. Todd's mixed-up metaphor reveals a crack in the oppressive reality that surrounds Joanna's world. There may not be a remedy to cure Joanna's mind in the world of the Fathers, but there may be in Mrs. Todd's world of the Mothers. Yet, the mixed metaphor also reveals the fact that Mrs. Todd's mediation of patriarchy has left her unable to adequately minister to Joanna's pain, or to fully understand the importance of Joanna's endeavor. Mrs. Todd, however, knows enough to honor her choice: "I never went to work to blame Joanna, as some did" (69), says Mrs. Todd. She lets go of Joanna and allows her to exist in her wild zone of femin(ine)ist existence.

In the wild zone of Shell-Heap Island, the rules are different: Joanna will not bow to patriarchal precepts, as is shown by her refusal to accept the coral pin from Mrs. Todd, which was purchased for Joanna by Mrs. Todd's husband, Nathan, "from a port he'd touched at somewheres up the Mediterranean" (70). Mrs. Todd acts symbolically as the go-between for patriarchy and the female world to bring his gift of the coral pin to Joanna. Yet Joanna, having gone through a "change" (70), refuses to accept it, for in doing so, she would be accepting an imprimatur of patriarchy, and she moved to Shell-Heap Island specifically to escape such fetters. A partial explanation of Joanna's rejection of the coral pin is that while it remains in the sea, coral is the "ocean's Tree of Life," which is the dwelling place of the Triple Goddess, the sea also being a symbolic wild zone (Walker, *Dictionary* 507, 472). In the ocean, coral is an indefinite, multiple, living organism that is dependent on others for its survival, much like Mrs. Todd's women's community. Taken out of the ocean, it dies. The removal of the coral from the ocean symbolizes for Joanna the terrible power of patriarchy to divide and conquer the worlds of women, as in some traditions, those who remove coral from the ocean are rewarded with the ability to "subdue all the three worlds," or those worlds inhabited by She-Who-Was, She-Who-Is, and She-Who-Will-Be—the three manifestations of the Goddess (511). Joanna recognizes that the coral in the pin is not symbolic of the living women's community, but is something that is dead: it has been transformed and fashioned by men into adornment. For Joanna, accepting the pin is accepting the economic and ornamental control of women by patriarchy, even in this small form.

The pin returns to Mrs. Todd's possession where it is kept for decades until it reappears again as a farewell gift for the narrator who leaves the shelter of the women's community of Dunnet Landing to return to the dark patriarchal world. Hence, Mrs. Todd's anger and frustration at the narrator's departure is manifested in the symbolic act of giving the coral pin to her at the end of the narrative. Significantly, the dead coral of the pin parallels the narrator's feeling that "I and all my belongings had died out of" Mrs. Todd's little house (Jewett 130). The pin metaphorically collapses the women's oral community of Dunnet Landing into the dead discourse of the narrator's tale that will be written in patriarchal words. Just as the coral dies after it has been wrested from its living existence in the ocean, so does the narrator's account of her vibrant experience atrophy into the anesthetized language of a written tale. What is left is simply a dead reminder of life, a textual puzzle that can be unlocked only by looking into its gaps to imagine what could have been if the language of patriarchy had not had the chance to possess and amend it—or if the narrator could reject that language in order to truly "return" to the world of women's words.

Jewett's narrative layering of the oscillating Demeter-Persephone myth with tales such as Joanna's represents the unstable success of a femin(ine)ist world independent from patriarchy. Thus, *The Country of the Pointed Firs* narrates cycles of femin(ine)ist becoming, where grandmothers, mothers, and daughters negotiate the difficulties of existing within patriarchy, creating productive lives without it, and letting go of daughters who are seduced by it—daughters who will eventually return to the safe spaces marked out by maternal elders who have also participated in this journey. As a fictional representation of this journey, Jewett's text allows readers to participate in the learning experience possible for them within the magical safety of women's words.

Like Sarah Orne Jewett, who focused on establishing a utopian woman-centered community as an alternative to the tyranny of patriarchy, Emma D. Kelley-Hawkins also used narrative as a way to create a space of mediation between patriarchal and femin(ine)ist realities. And like other black women writers of the late nineteenth century, Kelley-Hawkins participated in this task through an elucidation of black women's spirituality.[5] These were novels aimed at the world of middle-class African American women readers, and, because white publishing houses pressured authors to target as large a buying audience as possible, they were aimed at middle-class white women readers as well. As such, these novels served multiple purposes and operated on multiple levels. Just as *The Country of the Pointed Firs* creates a matrifocal alternative to androcentric urbanization, *Four Girls at Cottage City*, originally published in 1895 and reissued in 1898 due to its popularity, stands as a utopian retreat from the negativity and hardships of a racist patriarchal society in order to examine the lives of women (specifically, girls) within a woman-centered universe. Its idealized domestic and inward focus illustrates a utopian world parallel to Jewett's Dunnet Landing; as such, *Four Girls* is also key to an identification of the aesthetic threads of femin(ine)ist modernism.

While *The Country of the Pointed Firs* focuses on a metaphorical Demeter's world of Dunnet Landing, *Four Girls at Cottage City* shifts its focus from a symbolic Demeter to narrate Persephone's metaphorical attempt to elude the racist patriarchal underworld of urban America, to participate in the black matrifocal world of Cottage City's Trinity Park. Unlike Jewett's world of both mothers and daughters, however, the *Cottage City* girls are in a "modern condition" whereby daughters, as symbolic Persephones, are on their own in the process of their journey. They are urban New Women, educated in patriarchal traditions (at one point in the novel, the girls reveal that they attend normal school) and relatively alone in the world, as they work to create a women's community among themselves. Furthermore, the experiences of literature, mediums, spiritual guides, and scientists take the place of the direct experiential wisdom of Jewett's mothers, in the young women's attempt to negotiate a workable social position away from their mothers in the "underworld" of a racist, patriarchal society.

In contextualizing Kelley-Hawkins's narrative, it is important to recognize that, like Amelia Johnson's *The Hazeley Family* (1894), and Kelley-Hawkins's first novel, *Megda* (1891), *Four Girls at Cottage City* stands, similarly to Jewett's narrative, at the utopian beginning point in the cycle of women's narratives within femin(ine)ist modernism. The decade of the 1890s was one that saw an enlargement of literary production by black women, but one that also saw in the dominant culture a multiplication of racist ideas and an institutionalization of an American race caste system via the doctrine of "separate but equal" articulated in the case of *Plessy v. Ferguson* in 1896.[6] In the context of widespread racist attitudes, black women writers such as Kelley-Hawkins had a double task: to describe an artful and imagined, yet attainable, vision of the "Good" and "Just" life for black readers, while simultaneously dismantling stereotypes of black women held by white readers.

As Ann DuCille explains, a late-nineteenth-century concern for female moral authority resulted in the conflation of earlier literary techniques used by writers of the "race" or "romance" novel, so that "black women wrote another kind of novel in the 1890s" to focus their narrative attention on black women's spiritual needs (48). For authors such as Kelley-Hawkins, the evangelical allegory or domestic novel was a form of literature that could be used to enter into the intellectual and political debates of the era, while also creating an alternative to didactic discussions of the evils of slavery. As Claudia Tate explains, "These works also reflect the viewpoint widely held among turn-of-the-century African Americans that the acquisition of their full citizenship would result as much or more from demonstrating their adoption of the 'genteel standard of Victorian sexual conduct' as from protesting racial injustice" (4). By leaving out discussion of Civil War injustices, Kelley-Hawkins's novel marks a turn toward an idealized black femin(ine)ist reality in its vision of women of color in American society as "everyday" women whom readers (both black and white) might encounter in their daily activities. Furthermore, working within the tradition of the domestic novel allowed Kelley-Hawkins to carefully focus on a femin(ine)ist reality, one that DuCille explains is also "acutely concerned with issues of sisterhood and woman's community" (49).

In *Four Girls at Cottage City*, Kelly-Hawkins found her framework for sisterhood in an exploration of a subjective femin(ine)ist temporality through a resistance to racism within the tradition of the spiritual domestic narrative. Thus, her novel is feminine and interior, leaving traditional protest commentary to her literary sisters, as she aims her narrative at the growing body of black women readers seeking positive female role models in fictional characters. As Claudia Tate explains, this need for positive female role models in fiction is addressed by "female texts" such as *Four Girls* where "dominant discourses and their interpretations arise from woman-centered values, agency, indeed authority that seek distinctly female principles of narrative pleasure" (8). Accordingly, Kelley-Hawkins's novel is a femin(ine)ist narrative that focuses on themes inherent within the domestic lives of women of color, yet it is left ambiguous enough to appeal to white women as well.

Upon first reading *Four Girls*, one could easily miss the significance of the novel as a black woman's tale—indeed, Kelley-Hawkins may have purposely structured her novel that way. As Barbara Christian explains, literary conventions of the late nineteenth century dictated "a close correlation between physical type and spiritual qualities, at least in the area of woman images" (*Novelists* 22). Because nineteenth-century America structured its ideals of beauty on the white "lady," Christian theorizes that "the closest black women could come to such an ideal, at least physically, would of course have to be the mulatta, quadroon, or octoroon" (22). Moreover, this kind of character, according to DuCille, could help writers like Kelley-Hawkins attempt to subvert or surpass race categories: "'Whiteness' as Kelley uses it awkwardly but conventionally, is not so much a racial mark as an extended metaphor for spiritual purity in keeping with the text's and the genre's explicit concerns with religious salvation and the implied message that redemption transcends race. Since these texts are evangelical allegories and not romance or realism, the color of the characters may be less important than what their racelessness signifies" (54). Certainly, Kelley-Hawkins was participating in creating a kind of "white aesthetic" in order to be published, but could it be, too, that white readers are quick to identify the characters of *Four Girls* as white women simply because traditional (racist) education trains readers to identify characters as white by default? As DuCille asks, "what does it suggest about our interpretive needs as critics and our interpellation as subjects of racial ideology if we assume that figures not clearly identified as black or white are necessarily the latter?" (55). These questions point to the many complexities the reader encounters in the study of black women's fictional texts of the late nineteenth century, including those of Kelley-Hawkins.

*Four Girls at Cottage City* is a novel where the racial construction of characters is left to the imagination of the reader, black or white, as she builds images based on her lived experiences; but this is a literary strategy designed to, in Carole Watson's words, create "counter-stereotypes with whom white readers could identify" as part of a double-edged process to disrupt white notions of beauty and spirituality (13). Interestingly, Watson explains, "all of the heroes and heroines that appear in the race novels written before the First World War are fair-skinned mulattoes" (12). Kelley-Hawkins participates in this endeavor, creating characters in both *Megda* and *Four Girls* who are light-skinned "Do-Gooders," free of all but the most instructional of moral flaws. Like female characters in many nineteenth-century popular fictions, they are beautiful, smart, and good—girls any nineteenth-century woman reader would aspire to befriend.

In Kelley-Hawkins's novel, four young women, all of whom can be read as fair-skinned mulattoes, spend three weeks together on vacation at the resort town of Cottage City, which is modeled on the summer resort hamlet near Martha's Vineyard, Massachusetts, popular with the black middle class in the late nineteenth century. This setting, therefore, constitutes a subtle signal to black readers that Kelley-Hawkins's fictional subjects may not be white and, in fact, are probably light-skinned African American women able to "pass" as white. As Chris Stoddard explains, Cottage City (renamed Oak Bluffs in 1907) was generally receptive to African American visitors, and in the 1890s, "a number of boarding houses began to flourish catering to exclusively Black clientele" (102). Stoddard explains the development of Cottage City at the turn of the twentieth century: "Although this place was not immune to the various strains of racism and prejudice that have ailed our general society, their influence here has been tempered by local custom: the traditional and persistent tendency of Islanders to behave according to mores rooted in personal conviction rather than the fashion of the day. And Oak Bluffs, more than other Island towns, has had a history of being an ethnically mixed community. Year by year more friends and families came to stay, until Oak Bluffs had gained its reputation as the largest Black resort on the east coast" (102).

A typical femin(ine)ist text, Kelley-Hawkins's *Four Girls at Cottage City* confronts contradictions that work to destabilize the text, turning the "clear" patriarchal race categories of white, black, and mulatto on their heads, while simultaneously providing additional clues that the main characters of *Four Girls* are African American. Kelley-Hawkins creates this destabilization by exploding the category of mulatto, for one. She creates young heroines whose racial makeup participates in the literary tradition of the mulatta, which Brita Lindberg-Seyersted outlines as containing an explosive treatment of color: "Black writers have expanded on this meager palette [of only white, black, or mulatto] with an immense amount of creativity and with lots of humor and delight at a seemingly endless range of hues and shades, from darkest black to whitest near-white" (15). The heroines of *Four Girls* follow this continuum, with the darker women of the foursome, sisters Garnet and Jasmine (Jessie) Dare, described as having "rich complexions and dark eyes" (Kelley-Hawkins 15). Jasmine, the younger sister, has "big black eyes" (17) and a "dark" (15) or "black head" (18) crowned with "hair so thick" that it "seems impossible for a pin to go through it" (50). Jasmine's older sister, Garnet, has "great dark eyes" (10) and a "curly" (87) head of long hair. As Claudia Tate explains, the descriptions of both sisters are marked with "characteristics [that] reference African-American identity" (120). Their friend, Allie Hunt, is a "slender blue-eyed" (10) girl, with a "brown head" (18) and "pale face" (47), while Vera Earle is the lightest of the group, with her "grey eyes" (12) complemented by "red lips" (28), "golden hair" (47), and "white skin" (52). In spite of their fair coloring, it is evident that the girls' race is fixed as black in the white world. They have to sit for example, in "nigger heaven" (81) when they attend the theater. Significantly, Kelly-Hawkins emphasizes the lives of the "darker" women, sisters Jasmine and Garnet Dare, providing another marker of the girls' racialized positions that might have appealed to a readership of black women.

One key scene provides readers with yet another clue to the racial contradictions and complexities of the novel, as well as to a depiction of the fragility of Persephone's world carved out of the patriarchal underworld that still pushes in on them. Due to the racism of the period that rewards Vera's lighter skin color, she is pushed forward by the girls as the more "public" figure of the group, holding the girls' money in her purse as the "bank" (15) and taking the lead during their initial cottage-hunt upon arriving at Cottage City. Acting as the girls' agent, Vera knocks on the door to a cottage bearing the sign "Rooms to Let" and is immediately ushered in by "a pleasant-faced" white woman (26). But after she sees all the girls, the proprietor of this cottage does not seem eager to rent the rooms. When Vera asks if the group can be accommodated, the proprietor merely replies, "I think so" and leads them to "a pair of very steep, very narrow stairs," yet does not offer to show the girls the undesirable room at the top of the landing. Instead, she bows "a little stiffly," dismissing the girls to a "low, small room, which two narrow, dyspeptic looking beds almost entirely filled" (27). Clearly, the proprietor was willing to rent to a light-colored Vera, but changes her mind after she recognizes the more obvious race features of the other girls in the group.

Vera's dignified response to the insult models a feminine middle-class stratagem for surviving blows of racism well known to black readers: "Vera made a low bow towards the door, as though dismissing some person, and laid her 'belongings' on the floor. 'We'll bide here a bit, my maids,' she said drolly, 'before presenting our declination of the room to our friend in the lower regions. May the saints forgive me, but I'm very much thinking that her place in the after-life will be in the lower regions, if she has those kind of stairs put up for innocent people to break their necks upon'" (28). Certainly this is one scene, in Deborah McDowell's words, that is "rich with suggestion," giving readers a view of some of the earthly injustices the girls had hoped to escape during their vacation in Cottage City (xxvii). At any rate, the novel's sympathies are clear on the subject of racism, as it implies delicately that the "lower regions" are the only appropriate place in the afterlife for those who commit the sin of racism.

Kelley-Hawkins continues layering racial symbology into her narrative when she reveals that the girls eventually take residence in the same cottage—indeed, in the very room—where their heroine, Megda, spent the summer. An important point is that readers familiar with Kelley-Hawkins's previous novel *Megda* (1891) would recognize the reference to a work that was specifically promoted as a black woman's narrative, as the text of *Megda* was published with the author's photograph, showing her to be a serious and young, although light-skinned, African American woman. The girls' room is in "Trinity Park," and readers quickly recognize the Christian symbolism inherent in the name. But in terms of reading Persephone's world of *Four Girls*, Trinity Park also represents a much more feminized notion of the trinity as a symbol of the Goddess and her tripartite manifestations as virgin, mother, and crone. Befitting a feminine spiritual journey, the proprietor of the girls' Trinity Park cottage is an old crone called "Mother," who can be seen as symbolic of the goddess Hekate who accompanied Persephone on her underworld journey. She is attended by her husband-servant, old Mr. Atherton, who welcomes the virginal group to lodgings seeped in matricity, occupied as they once were by Net and Jessie Dare with their mother several years earlier.

Signaling "Mother's" role as crone, Vera notes that she is evidently "the ruling spirit" of the house, and the girls immediately take a liking to the establishment (31). Their first glimpse of "Mother" establishes her dominance over her husband, echoing Mrs. Todd's intermediary role in restraining male influence over the women in Dunnet Landing: "Four fair, girlish faces, were turned expectantly toward the spot where she stood; four pair of bright, girlish eyes, were lifted to her face; and four warm, impulsive, girlish hearts, were at once laid at the trembling feet of 'mother.' But even while the girls looked at, and loved at once, the pale, refined, gentle old face, framed with its soft waves of silvery hair, they couldn't help noticing, that while one slender hand patted nervously the pale blue cap that had evidently been put on hurriedly, the other rested on the arm of, and held determinedly back, her husband" (31). In this scene is a female world established as a place of safety for the girls, preserved and sustained by the wise crone "Mother." Mother's power here is complete, the girls notice, as "Grandpa" Atherton is relegated to a constant position of "peering at them over 'Mother's' shoulder" (36, 41–42).

The text emphasizes "Mother's" control of "Grandpa" when Vera asks, "Girls, how long do you suppose 'Mother' has been holding 'Grandpa' back with that little slender hand of hers?" (42). They discuss the power of the crone to keep men at bay:

> "I guess she commenced holding him back when the question as to who should rule was first brought up," said Garnet, disappearing into one of the closets to hand her dress up.
>
> "'Grandpa' seems to yield to it pretty well," said Allie from the other closet.
>
> "Yes, 'Mother's' victory seems to have been complete," said Vera, sitting down on the bed and beginning to unbutton her boots. "Who would imagine such a will-power in a delicate body like her. And such a hand as *she* has! Truly it is a 'velvet hand in an iron *glove*.'" (42–43; Kelley-Hawkins's emphasis)

Just as Mrs. Todd's Demeter provides a refuge for the narrator of *Pointed Firs*, "Mother" as a figure of Hekate provides a space of refuge within the underworld of patriarchy for the girls of *Cottage City*. Interestingly, some versions of the Demeter-Persephone myth name Hekate as Persephone's attendant and companion as she resided in the underworld. Unlike the world of Mrs. Todd, however, male danger is more immediate here; hence, crone Hekate must govern with more force. The girls recognize the power inherent in "Mother's" rule, yet they chafe a bit under the generational hierarchy commanded by the crone. In this way, *Four Girls* makes a distinct social-historical break here, signaling a change in black women's literary aesthetics, as the conflict for the girls of the novel is both racial *and* generational, framed by the complexities of gender. Here, Kelley-Hawkins skillfully highlights the girls' interaction with their elders and comrades to show a new kind of conflict faced by modern young women at the turn of the twentieth century. These are girls who are out on their own, walking freely in public places without obvious chaperones, and making decisions about their lives without input from their elders. Unlike Jewett's Persephone-narrator of *Pointed Firs*, who spends time isolated within the safe confines of the women's community of Dunnet Landing before she goes out to find her way in the underworld of patriarchy, these young Persephones have instead briefly found their way out of the patriarchal underworld to return to the matrifocal environment of Trinity Park. In the space of the story, the four girls' journey is eased by the presence of the attendant crone Hekate, as they are temporarily removed from the full force of not only patriarchal society, but also white society, by the crone's somewhat more manageable environment at Trinity Park.

Separated from their mothers, the girls find their way to this matrifocal stopping point together, but it cannot be a complete place of refuge, as it is complicated by interruptions of male society. Jess identifies these interruptions in her irritation with the frequent social advances of cousin Fred and his friend, Mr. Erfort Richards, into the fragile women's world of Trinity Park. The women's community is to Jess's liking, and she soon tires of the male intrusion as an unneeded and avoidable harassment. Eventually, an argument breaks out between Jess and her companions over attending a band concert with the men, where Jess articulates her frustration with male intrusion into her world of women: "I'm not going because I'm tired to death of having those two fellows tied to our apron strings everywhere we go. We can't move but what 'the *gen-tle-men* will *call* for us at such and *such* a time.' I'm tired to death of it. When we came down here I thought we four girls were going around together and have a good time. There's no fun when there's a parcel of men around. I wont [*sic*] go out with them again—see if I do. I'll stay cooped up in the this room all the time I'm here, first" (129; Kelley-Hawkins's emphasis).

Jess seethes at the fact that Fred and Erfort have crossed from the periphery of the girls' world into the center of it. If anything, Jess's outburst against the men reveals that she had expected to be free of at least the sexual oppression of overattendant men; moreover, their vacation destination (popular with black tourists) reveals that the girls also hoped to be spared episodes of race oppression. Likewise, the fact that the girls chose to journey on their own (without adult chaperones) shows that they had planned to be free of generational oppressions, as well. Importantly, this scene lays the groundwork for the female subversion of male privilege that will ultimately conclude the narrative.

Jasmine's anger at male intrusion causes her to transform into a "wicked little sprite" (133) able to strike the men speechless, and it is at this point that Jasmine's raw power as an uninitiated sibyl (perhaps a younger, untrained version of Mrs. Todd) is brought out: "They saw a little white face, lighted by two brilliant black eyes and crowned with a mass of dark hair, peering eerily down at them through the branches of the big tree. They raised their hats, but neither spoke" (133). Jess symbolically takes command of the storytelling at this point, transforming the narrative from its emphasis on the interaction between the men and the women to, in essence, one that strikes the men speechless. Thus begins the novel's weaving of a woman's tale focusing on the women's community of the girls and their spiritual mentor.

This woman's tale is Charlotte's story, and it parallels Joanna's tale in *The Country of the Pointed Firs*. It is initiated by Vera's observation of Charlotte at morning tabernacle services and fleshed out by Jess's visits to Charlotte's small cottage, significantly situated on the edge of town, another female wild zone. The story of the mulatta washerwoman, Charlotte Mehitable Phillips Chase Hood, and her son Robin, like that in Jewett's story, serves as an allegory for life as it will be for modernist women. Like Joanna's, Charlotte's story is of a woman who has been alienated from life in the patriarchal underworld, a parable of the trials and tribulations of women under patriarchy told to the four girls in an effort to "save" them—both religiously (the surface story) and from the cross of patriarchy (the subsurface story). Using the narrative technique of multiple inversions, Charlotte's account builds a new female-centered story of Christianity, showing, as Claudia Tate explains, "that the way to Christ is mediated by women" (177). Charlotte, too, is a

Persephone figure who serves as a successful role model for the youthful Persephones of the four girls; but in Charlotte, the four girls meet a woman who has journeyed alone through the patriarchal underworld, and by the strength of her spiritual resources and solidarity with women, has returned—or been resurrected—to the land of the living.

Like Jewett who rewrites the classical myth of Demeter and Persephone, Kelley-Hawkins deploys spiritual feminism to rewrite the social myth of patriarchal Christianity in order to displace a masculine Christ with a feminine one in the form of Charlotte as Persephone. Even the name Charlotte is a kind of feminine homonym for Christ, and both are "washers," for in Christian doctrine, Christ "washes us from our sins with his own blood" (Rev. 1:5), while Charlotte's task in *Four Girls* is not only to wash the garments of the residents of Cottage City (93, 96) but also to wash the hearts of the four girls clean from sin. In this capacity, Charlotte displaces the traditional Christian trinity; however, here the father-figure is eliminated instead of the mother-figure, and the son is crippled by severe and unending pain, waiting to be saved by the charitable women's work of the girls at the end of the novel, again reinforcing the theme of salvation through the mediation of women.

As a spiritual guide, Charlotte becomes a fixation for the girls, who seek a mentor to teach them the ways of making their journey through the patriarchal underworld. In the first installment of Charlotte's narrative, readers learn that she is "chosen by God," but for what remains unclear. As readers are drawn deeper into Charlotte's trials and tribulations, they learn with the girls that she had become a "woman of the world" as she descended into the underworld of despair and hardship, until she is transformed by a provocative and mystical dream. In the dream, Charlotte tells of a vision of many sinners, including the inept and dull parson who did not minister to her during her time of trouble when her family was sick with the fever. It is important to note that Charlotte states that her dream is framed by the experience of reading a woman's novel: "I dreamed that I was dead and on my journey to my future home. I thought that the three days when I was lying dead [in] my home were the three days that it took me to perform the journey. I passed through many scenes—somewhat similar to those described by Elizabeth Stuart Phelps in 'Beyond the Gates'" (299). Charlotte's reference to Phelps signals once again the power of women's narrative, a power that she, too, hopes to tap in her story for the four girls. Moreover, the initial experience of Charlotte's life shows her that the patriarchal God is hard-hearted and unmerciful, while his male servants (symbolized in the form of the parson) are ineffectual.

But in this woman's dream-tale of heaven, God the harsh judge and father is transformed into the loving parent who lifts the "poor old woman" (299), Hester Norton, to a place of glory at His right hand while condemning the Parson for "the most unpardonable sin of all," because he "preached the Word falsely" (315). Interestingly, the Reverend's "unpardonable sin" is analogous to the "unpardonable sin" of Jewett's Joanna—but with a twist. In Jewett's hint at the dystopian future, Joanna is punished (or silenced) for her anger against patriarchy, while in Kelley-Hawkins's idealized realm, the Reverend is condemned for corrupting what could be most liberating for women: the Word. This statement in *Four Girls*, in some ways, is the most explosive of the novel, for it snatches away the power of patriarchal discourse and transforms it into the primary form of femin(ine)ist power—the power of Women's Words. It is through the power of women's words that Charlotte's story is an allegory of reinvention in Persephone's return—a staple in the aesthetic of femin(ine)ist modernism that transforms patriarchal stories and myths into femin(ine)ist ones. After metaphorically "eating" the pomegranate seed of white patriarchal knowledge and experiences, Charlotte returns to a woman-centered word/world. Thus, Charlotte becomes a female redeemer who survives her journey through the hardships of a racist and sexist underworld to be reunited with the women's world of the four girls.

Although *Four Girls at Cottage City* essentially structures two endings—the first being the girls' departure from the haven of Trinity Park to return to their underworld journey, the second being the obligatory marriage ending of the sentimental novel—it is the first ending that fits most closely with the metaphorical structure of the narrative. Interestingly, *Four Girls at Cottage City* parallels the conclusion to Jewett's *The Country of the Pointed Firs* in that the departing Persephones are each given a gift by their mediating hosts that is symbolic of the dual nature of living within, yet without, patriarchy. Jewett's narrator is given the coral pin that "poor Joanna" rejected by her host Mrs. Todd (131), while the four girls are each given "a neat black testament" by "Mother" Atherton (369). These gifts, then, become charms given by magical mediators to protect the young Persephones on their journeys—a kind of "passport," if you will, that guarantees their safe passage through the patriarchal underworld. While they are at once fetishes of patriarchy—designed not to draw attention to their holders—the coral pin is representative of patriarchal ornamentation and control, while the Bibles given to the girls are representative of patriarchal spirituality; these talismans simultaneously carry with them a shared secret meaning that reminds the wandering Persephones of their maternal givers.[7] Thus, as the young Persephones leave their sacred and safe places to continue their cyclical journey, they carry closely with them a magical reminder of the power of women, occulted under cover of patriarchal objects, just as their communities of safety are hidden within the patriarchal world.

As mystical mediators, Mrs. Todd of *The Country of the Pointed Firs* and Charlotte Hood and Mother Atherton of *Four Girls of Cottage City* are able to mediate patriarchy to carve out a world where women can patiently exist as they wait for their Persephones to return, while their connection to Demeter's mother-knowledge allows them to show their Persephone-daughters the way through other worlds, guided through the power of women's words. As reconstructions of the Demeter-Persephone myth, *The Country of the Pointed Firs* and *Four Girls at Cottage City* provide an idealized alternative to the tyranny of the patriarchal underworld, but more important, the myth of Demeter and Persephone also reveals how even a powerful goddess like Demeter is still bound by patriarchal conventions. Her power remains limited, as she operates "from the margins, using the last resort of the weak, [her] nonviolent noncooperation" (Hayes 14). Hence, the encoded tales of the women of *The Country of the Pointed Firs* and *Four Girls at Cottage City* portray the paradox of choices available to Demeter-women living within the racism and sexism of patriarchy, sketching the possibilities within its gaps, utopianly beyond its censure.

By harnessing the metaphorical power of the myths of Demeter-Persephone and Christianity, Jewett and Kelley-Hawkins are able to plumb the depths of both gender and race relations between women and men, whites and blacks, at the close of the nineteenth century. Thus, both novels develop a textual space that exists in the gap between traditional masculine realism and the dystopian tradition of female modernism; nevertheless, they are texts that reflect the ambivalence of femin(ine)ist modernism, as they can explore, yet cannot completely violate, established boundaries of gender, race, class, and ideology. Instead, their embedded acknowledgment of contradictions establishes a framework for subversion that femin(ine)ist modernists develop more fully in later decades. Although the texts' utopian surfaces might at first glance seem to reveal an idyllic woman's existence, the uncertainty of Persephone's journey through the patriarchal underworld presses in upon these texts, hinting at the isolation awaiting women at the turn of the twentieth century.

# 4

# Aphrodite's Fall

*Aphrodite, Undine, and Andromeda in the Works of Onoto Watanna, Alice Dunbar-Nelson, and Edith Wharton*

\* Onoto Watanna (b. 1875), Alice Dunbar-Nelson (b. 1875), and Edith Wharton (b. 1862) are members of the second generation of women analyzed in this study. The women of this generation were born during a period of American economic dominance and came of age in America's Gilded Age, when Populists and Suffragists took political center stage from war hawks and doves, and where discussions of black enfranchisement entered into political debates. Their generation included women such as Ida B. Wells-Barnett, Sui Sin Far, Willa Cather, Gertrude Stein, Natalie Barney, Angelina Weld Grimké, Jessie Fauset, and Anne Spencer. Their coming of age was ushered in by the 1886 Haymarket Riots, discussions of the New Woman, and the broadminded social organizations of women's clubs and settlement houses. As young adults, these women witnessed waves of immigration and new virulent expressions of racism in the years before the turn of the twentieth century, as well as America's culture of institutional racism in the passage of the Chinese Exclusion Act (1882) and the reification of the doctrine of "separate but equal" in *Plessy v. Ferguson* (1896). This was the generation made up of the children of the post–Civil War era who were confident enough to take advantage of new educational, economic, and spiritual opportunities with which to explore their horizons.

While Sarah Orne Jewett and Emma Kelley-Hawkins illuminated Demeter's world of powerful mothers and sheltered daughters, the reality of fin-de-siècle America was that it moved quickly toward a new century and a new social order—one that threatened to seduce the daughters of the first generation. As Josephine Donovan explains, "Like Demeter, late nineteenth century mothers were struggling to keep their daughters 'home,' thereby sustaining women's culture. [...] the daughters, on the other hand, were eager to expand their horizons, to engage in new systems of discourse, like Persephone, unaware that such involvement entailed patriarchal captivity" (*After the Fall* 44). But once out in the twentieth century (under)world, Persephone finds herself isolated from her mother's world. Torn from her matrifocal realm, she sheds her mother's bond and her pastoral position as Persephone to become Aphrodite: a woman of the world. Accordingly, Persephone's transformation represents not simply an adolescent rebellion against her mother, but the end result of being lured from the halcyon world of her mother's garden into the modern, twinkling, patriarchal city.

Late-nineteenth- and early-twentieth-century industrialization and urbanization saw women, along with millions of other Americans, move from farm-centered lifestyles in rural areas to pursue new opportunities in the cities as factory workers, clerks, and shop girls. For many women these social and economic changes were positive, but for others they were negative. Dorothy and Carl J. Schneider explain that "The urbanization that sent America's people from its countryside to its cities cost many women their established support systems. Alone, or with their husbands and children, they left behind their sisters and their mothers and their aunts, their neighborhoods where everyone spoke on the street and everyone helped her neighbors. They moved from farms or small towns where everyone knew their antecedents and status to the indifference of the city. For some, it was alienation—for others, liberation" (5). For many young women, the city offered a new way of living: one that was free from the prying eyes of family or neighbors, and one that catered to their youthful desires in the form of dance halls and opera halls, department stores, and "apartment hotels that freed them from domestic cares" (5). This was a lifestyle that allowed a young woman to focus on herself to indulge her needs and desires. But for as many women as urbanization liberated, it imprisoned more. Many who had come to the city expecting to find financial freedom and social liberation in a meaningful profession found instead that they had been sentenced "to long hours and dull, repetitious labor in dead-end jobs that kept them far below the poverty level" (5). What was good for one woman might not be good for another.

One of the most dramatic changes that took place for women at the turn of the twentieth century was the change in social codes governing sexual activity. Indeed, the oft-quoted phrase from the periodical *Current Opinion* was the 1913 phrase that the clock had struck "Sex O'clock in America" (Schneider and Schneider 137). Certainly, many of the old rules governing out-of-wedlock births and sexual promiscuity were in place, but the early years of the twentieth century had ushered in a new era governing sexual relationships. For example, Schneider and Schneider explain that "Younger women were more frequently indulging in premarital and extramarital sex than their foremothers," and radicals in the wake of infamous personalities such as Victoria Woodhull advocated free love (142). But this new-found freedom was not without cost for these women. Schneider and Schneider explain:

> In factories, laundries, restaurants, and department stores their co-workers talked openly of their romances and their sexuality, exchanging risqué jokes, smutty cards, and sexual advice. Their workplaces afforded little or no privacy. The sexual aspersions and invitations of their male co-workers constantly belittled them. Their bosses—whether foremen or floorwalkers—often demanded sexual favors as the price of promotion or indeed of just keeping their jobs. Male customers at restaurants often left their cards, and waitresses knew that responding brought good tips. Low wages forced working women to some form of supplementing their wardrobes or their income. (144)

Working women who earned only a small percentage of working men's wages could not often afford the steep price of admission to popular places of entertainment. Schneider and Schneider explain that "if they wanted 'treats' like food and drink, the men they met must provide them. Some women entered the competition for male attention with low décolletages, gauze stockings, high-heeled shoes, extravagantly decorated hats, and 'rats' or 'puffs' in their hair" (145). Style and sexuality, then, became the currency of choice for these New Women who had begun the transformation from pastoral Persephones who eschewed male company for the homosocial world of women, to city-wise, sexual Aphrodites who openly embraced men and their world.

Consequently, the idealized evocation of Demeter and Persephone in late-nineteenth-century femin(ine)ist fiction now turns and is ruled by a figure, based on the goddess Aphrodite, who struggles to forge an existence in the world of men. As readers may recall, Aphrodite is the "immortal blend of heavenly perfection and mortal fallibility," signifying the union of the idealized heaven of Demeter's matristic worlds with the fallibility of women's lives under patriarchy (Bell 53). But this simple mythography tends to shy away from the more complex issues of violence, liminality, and sexuality evoked in the story of Aphrodite's birth. Specifically, she was born when the Titan Uranus was castrated by his son Cronus, who then threw the severed genitals into the ocean. From this bloody tempest, the ocean began to churn and spume—and from this chaos Aphrodite was born, rising naked out of the foam. Joanne H. Stroud tells the story: "Aphrodite emerges with the pearlescent dawn, clothed in hues of pink and aqua, an ephemeral beauty visible for a few radiant moments as darkness lingers at the cusp of the heavens, soon to be eclipsed by the incandescent light of day. She is always on the margin—of day and night, of sea and shore. She is the misty fusion of water and air in the luminescent sea foam or morning dew" (104). As Stroud explains, "Aphrodite is always betwixt and between places, both spatially and emotionally. Her proximity signifies a possible turning, a moment of change, a transformation" (106). Thus, the circumstances of her birth associate Aphrodite with the eternal oscillation of sex and death, as well as her liminal position of being not of the sea (associated with Woman) nor land (associated with Man), not of night (darkness) nor day (light), but of something more abstruse and in-between.

According to Paul Friedrich, like the goddess Athena who was also created whole, Aphrodite's emergence as an absolute being symbolizes "the intimate relation of each goddess with her father and, by extension, with males generally [...]. Both, thus, are strongly identified with their father, and each, in her way, symbolized the denial of the mother" (82). Hence, Aphrodite's identification with her father echoes the position of early-twentieth-century daughters who distanced themselves from their mothers in order to move from one century into the next. This generation's Aphrodites, however, were like Persephone in that their moment of change was abrupt (as was Persephone's abduction) as well as incomplete. Unable to forge a completely distinct identity from their mothers, they were influenced greatly by the new world of the fathers, yet unable to become completely immersed in it. Thus, Aphrodite exists as a liminal figure—a woman looking simultaneously to opposite worlds, yet unable to fully exist in either. This image of Aphrodite as a woman between two worlds works especially well as an overriding metaphor for a discussion of the turn-of-the-twentieth-century transition point in femin(ine)ist fiction, as the authors discussed in this chapter—Onoto Watanna, Alice Dunbar-Nelson, and Edith Wharton—seem to be entangled in a "between-world" haunted by the utopian shadow of their literary foremothers, yet dominated by rigid patriarchal definitions of Woman. As a result, the turn of the twentieth century was for these women a paradox: it was a world that imposed strict restrictions on both white women and women of color regarding their choice of occupation, where they lived, and with whom they socialized, yet simultaneously offered the promises of social and economic freedom in a new urban world.

Appropriately, this tension is found in classical Aphrodite's story. Although traditional birth myths focus on Aphrodite's rejection of her maternal parentage, Aphrodite is also called "Mari" or "the sea" in some legends (Walker, *Encyclopedia* 44–45), linking her symbolically to her ever-present, yet unseen mother—much like late-nineteenth- and early-twentieth-century authors were linked to their nineteenth-century literary mothers. For example, the authors discussed in this chapter were influenced by the elucidation of women's communities in the fiction of their nineteenth-century foremothers; yet, they were also women who attempted to separate themselves from those communities as they looked toward lives as independent "New Women" of the twentieth century.

In the more woman-centered myths of Aphrodite, she appears as the first offspring of the primal Mother (as water) in the form of a water-spirit or mermaid, or in her wicked nymph form as an Undine.[1] It is in these legends, highlighting Aphrodite's liminal form as a water sprite, that she is most closely linked to the women writers at the dawn of the twentieth century.[2] Aphrodite/Undine is a woman on her own in the world of men, who enjoys male society, glamour, fashion, and the sensual experiences of the body. She is bright and changeable, adapting to situations that hold her fancy, but these qualities also lend to her personality a shallowness, because she avoids deep emotions for the thrill of being in love. She can be vague, restless, and irresponsible, as she needs constant change to support her amusements. Her darker side shows the folly of toying with Aphrodite's power, for the reason that her pleasures could easily and quickly be turned to violent and creative torments. As the fallen nymph Undine, her sexual powers are avaricious and robust, reminding readers of the mythological origins of the term *nymphomaniac*.

The complexities sketched briefly above are important to any metaphorical discussion of Aphrodite, as "the distinctively Greek mythic breakup of 'the feminine' into contrasting features and functions" mirrors late-nineteenth- and early-twentieth-century androcentric literary traditions that also fragment the feminine (Friedrich 72). But on a more liberatory note, these were often the very fragmentations that were the aspects of the Goddess invoked by femin(ine)ist authors such as Onoto Watanna in *Miss Nume of Japan* (1899), Alice Dunbar-Nelson in *A Modern Undine* (c. 1900), and Edith Wharton in *The House of Mirth* (1905) and *The Custom of the Country* (1913). The four texts examined in this chapter investigate the fragmentation of Aphrodite from her position as the sensual love-goddess in the form of Onoto Watanna's Nume, who struggles with her alter ego Cleo Ballard as an Undine figure; to the story of Aphrodite's fall from power and grace in the form of Dunbar-Nelson's Marion and Wharton's Lily Bart; to her most vital, powerful, and sexually manipulative form as Undine in the form of Wharton's Undine Spragg. As a trope for the twentieth century's New Woman, Aphrodite's fall from a masculine pedestal of sensual grace to the form of a sexual, self-indulgent, survivalist Undine sets the stage for the disintegration of the "feminine" in later modernist texts.

Onoto Watanna's *Miss Nume of Japan* (1899) provides a starting point for the discussion of Aphrodite's fall from patriarchy's grace, as it provides a glimpse of her double manifestations in the tragic love story of two Americans and two Japanese. Written during her residence in Chicago, *Miss Nume of Japan* was Winnifred Eaton's first novel and was published under the nom de plume Onoto Watanna.[3] The novel was successful enough that it was followed by twelve other novels and numerous short fiction pieces. Like William Faulkner, Eaton's popularity as a novelist earned her a career in Hollywood working on movie scripts during the 1920s, where she was eventually made head of Universal Studio's scenario department (Ling, "Winnifred Eaton" 6).

Born the middle child to an English father and Chinese mother, Eaton's rejection of her Chinese heritage for Japanese, as well as her popularity as a romance novelist, has caused contemporary critics to slight Onoto Watanna, favoring instead her sister who published under the Chinese pseudonym Sui Sin Far. Born in Montreal and spending much of her adult life in America, Watanna never traveled to Japan, relying instead on research, reading, and popular American images of Japan as inspiration for her novels. As Amy Ling explains, "her keen marketing instinct and sense of timing were precisely accurate, for orientalism was in full flower at the turn of the century" ("Creating One's Self" 310). By tapping into the popular culture of the time, Watanna was able to capitalize on her ambiguous ethnic heritage, boosting her novelistic success to command up to $15,000 advance royalty before publication as well as a significant share of post-publication royalties. As Ling explains, Onoto Watanna's popularity at the height of her career allowed her to circulate with literary luminaries such as Edith Wharton and Mark Twain (*Between Worlds* 29).

Watanna's popularity was solidified through her use of romantic narrative. Her first novel, *Miss Nume of Japan*, is a story of star-crossed interracial love between Takashima Orito, a Harvard-educated Japanese man, and a white American woman Cleo Ballard. As readers venture into the novel, they learn of another interracial pair: Nume, the innocent promised bride of Orito, and Arthur Sinclair, who is an American diplomat and Cleo's fiancé. Through the machinations of the plot, the four lovers move together and pull apart, resulting in the suicide of Orito, the marriage of Nume and Sinclair, and the exit of Cleo from Japan to America, where she weds her longtime friend and cousin Tom Ballard. Certainly this is a lover's trap worthy of the exotic Aphrodite's attention, and consistent with the trope of Aphrodite, Watanna skillfully reconstructs and problematizes race as more than romantically exotic in order to complicate her interracial lover's quadrangle. In the romance, race is not *erased,* as both Orito and Nume are specifically marked as Asian characters, although they are marked by playing off of American cultural clichés. Because Watanna works with America's early-twentieth-century stereotypes, readers would have identified with the pre–World War II romanticization of Japanese women as guileless, simple, and exotically beautiful, and the American characters as worldly and powerful. For example, Nume, the exotic and feminine woman is romanticized as pure, innocent, childlike, and beautiful—a perfect stereotypical romantic pairing for the masculine and powerful American Arthur Sinclair.

Readers are first introduced to Nume at the beginning of the novel, and although after her introduction Nume is not heard from until the second quarter of the romance, she haunts the margins of the novel: "Now Nume was a very peculiar child. Unlike most Japanese maidens, she was impetuous and wayward. Her mother had died when she was born, and she had never had any one to guide or direct her, so that she had grown up in a careless, happy fashion, worshiped by her father's servants, but depending entirely upon

Orito for all her small joys. [. . .] Orito loved Nume because she was one day to be his little wife, and because she was very bright and pretty; whilst Nume loved big Orito with a pride that was pathetic in its confidence" (7–8). In addition to alluding to a life without a mother, as Aphrodite had faced, Nume's description is tinged with aspects of the American New Woman's personality in the fact that she is "unlike most Japanese maidens" and that she is both "impetuous and wayward." Nume is the ingenuous child-bride promised to Orito at the beginning of the novel, before he sails for a sophisticated Harvard education in America. Unlike Orito, who loves out of duty, Nume loves because love is her very essence—it needs only to be directed by the men in her life, her father and fiancé. From the beginning of the narrative, Nume is cast as Aphrodite in her form as a patriarchal love-goddess. As the novel discloses, "Nume" means plum blossom in Japanese (9), associating Nume with both Aphrodite and love itself, for it is the fruit of plum trees, itself a sexual symbol, that is eaten to inspire or maintain love (Cunningham 180).

Nume's foil is Cleo Ballard, who is also a metaphorical aspect of Aphrodite. Cleo's first name can be seen as a homonym for that of Cleio who is one of the nine muses, typically symbolized as the "proclaimer" or inspirational muse of history and tale-telling, while Cleo's last name, Ballard, can be seen as a homonym for Cleio's ballads. Cleio is also named as a goddess of springs and streams, thus associating her, like Aphrodite, with water (Cleio's symbolizing apparatus is the clepsydra, or a device that measures time by marking the regulated flow of water). As a more worldly fragment of Aphrodite, Cleo is said to have "laughed at Aphrodite for her infatuation with the mortal Adonis" (Tripp 89). Moreover, Cleo's most ancient aspects identify her, like Aphrodite, as a manifestation of the Triple Goddess—the Triple Goddess, of course, being the principle figure who haunts the margins of femin(ine)ist fiction (Farrar and Farrar 250).

As befits her standing as a demigoddess associated with water, readers first encounter Cleo on a transoceanic steamer traveling from America to Japan. Significantly, Cleo stands at the ship's rail, gazing out to sea as if to imitate mariners' practice of placing a woman's figure at the prow of a ship: "A sudden wind came up from the sea and caught the red cape she wore, blowing it wildly about her" (12). The red cape, of course, signifies her divine passionate power. The novel then pauses to give a lengthy description of Cleo, one that draws upon Aphrodite's aspects as an Undine:

Cleo Ballard was a coquette; such an alluring, bright, sweet, dangerous coquette. She could not have counted her adorers, because they would have included every one who knew her. Such a gay, happy girl as she was; always looking about her for happiness, and finding it only in the admiration and adoration of her victims; for they were victims, after all, because, though they were generally willing to adore in the beginning, she nevertheless crushed their hopes in the end; for that is the nature of coquettes. Hers was a strange, paradoxical nature. She would put herself out, perhaps go miles out of the way, for the sake of a new adorer, one whose heart she knew she would storm, and then perhaps break. She would do this gayly, thoughtlessly, as unscrupulously and impetuously as she tore the little silk gloves from her hands because they came not off easily. [. . .] With a laugh she pulled the heart-strings till they ached with pain and pleasure commingled; but when the poor heart burst with the tension, then she would run shivering away, and hide herself, because so long as she did not see the pain she did not feel it. (15–16)

Cleo's description turns on the more negative aspects of Aphrodite, suggesting her transmogrified form as an Undine. Like the goddess Aphrodite, Cleo's "eyes were dark blue, sombre, gentle eyes at times, wicked, mischievous, mocking eyes at others" (16) signifying her association with the sea. Cleo's description also alludes to Aphrodite's golden physicality, as she "had sun-kissed, golden-brown hair—dark brown at night and in the shadow, bright gold in the daytime and in the light" (16), with the changeability of her hair color further indicating Cleo's power as a metaphorical Undine to transform according to circumstance.[4]

As Aphrodite's more physical and sexual evocation, Cleo embodies one side of the goddess's form as the nymph Undine—a creature who is driven to attach herself to men, due to the fact that an undine's power is gained through male adoration, and without it, she withers and dies. This becomes quite clear from the novel's description of Cleo's relationship with Orito on the steamer: "The man's homage intoxicated Cleo. She knew all the men worth knowing on board—had known many of them in America. She had tired, bored herself, flirting with them. It was a refreshment to her now to wake the admiration—the sentiment—of this young Japanese, because they had told her he always concealed his emotions so skillfully. [. . .] She could not help it that he admired her, she told herself, and admiration and homage were to her what the sun and rain is to the flowers" (22). Without the company of her fiancé, Sinclair, Cleo is instantly drawn to the man on board who would present her the most interesting amorous challenge. Thus, Cleo spends the duration of her time aboard ship positioning Orito as a helpless lover. Eventually, Orito tells Cleo of his engagement to Nume—marriage plans that are without romantic love—and asks Cleo to marry him. Cleo, consumed "with an almost feverish longing for his companionship and sympathy" (52), does not reveal her own engagement to Sinclair and allows Orito to believe she will become engaged to him at the journey's end. As the shores of Japan come into view, Orito declares, "Soon we will reach home now—your home and mine" (53), driving Cleo into a panic. Although, like Sinclair, Orito is a wealthy and well-educated man, Cleo's racism prevents her from accepting his proposal. Unwilling to risk the displeasure of her family, she seeks instead her own passing pleasure through a relationship she has no intention of consummating.

Thus, the novel establishes Cleo as a sexual and unfaithful Undine who trifles with men in pursuit of her own pleasure. Here Cleo is represented as the New Woman qua femme fatale, a portrayal of women quickly castigated by feminist critics when similar characters are portrayed by male writers. Why would Onoto Watanna—a New Woman herself—choose to present such a negative characterization of a woman? Like similar characters in the fiction of Alice Dunbar-Nelson and Edith Wharton, the feminine femme fatale raises disturbing questions and contradictory answers for contemporary feminist critics. One answer to these difficult and complex questions might lie in Watanna's portrayal of Cleo as something more than a static, evil figure, which is typically how androcentric literature portrays the femme fatale. In *Miss Nume of Japan,* Cleo begins her romantic (and literal) journey as a coquette; however, her journey ends as a heartbroken woman who has lost her lover. Certainly, Cleo's behavior during the first two-thirds of the novel is irresponsible and self-indulgent, as she enjoys using Undine's power to play with men; but toward the end of the novel, Cleo's breakdown and "lovesickness" parallels Nume's, revealing a woman who has both a conscience and a heart.

Thus, Cleo is not a simple femme fatale; she is a woman who has gone through a journey of the heart, revealing Watanna's intertwined explorations of love and racism. As Cleo explains at the end of the narrative, "*He* [Orito] was better than the other [Sinclair]. So much tenderer and truer—the best man I ever knew—the only person in the whole world who ever really loved me. And I [. . .], I *killed* him!" (209; Watanna's emphasis). As a moral love tale, Cleo's story in *Miss Nume of Japan* portrays the chilling repercussions of racism in relationships, while Nume's story portrays Watanna's main theme that love is stronger than both race or class status. In this view, it is useful to examine Sinclair's character as a kind of hinge linking the two love stories. Echoing Cleo's racism that prevents her from openly loving Orito, Sinclair overcomes his racism to fall in love with and marry Nume, thus completing the overriding didactic tale that "love conquers all." Viewed in this manner, Cleo is no longer a vicious femme fatale; instead, she becomes a nontraditional, although confused, Undine who at the end of the narrative realizes that she does not want to break hearts and turns instead into a better woman who has begun her journey back to her form as the more sensitive Aphrodite.

In contrast to Cleo's characterization as an Undine, Nume is characterized as a kind of male fantasy Aphrodite, the quintessential goddess of love who shapes herself to male desire. She is natural, beautiful, and simple, and loves/lives only to please others. Watanna writes, "When the Americans had settled so near her home, the girl had gone out curiously among them, studying their strange manners and customs, learning to speak their language, and often seen dressing in their costume, to the amusement of her father, Sachi, and the Americans. They had sought her out in the beginning because of her extraordinary beauty" (65). Nume is love personified in its most pure and untainted aspects, and unlike Cleo's Undine, Nume has a soul and her soul is Love. While Cleo lives as a kind of love parasite, Nume lives through the love she spreads among others, inspired and maintained through her extraordinary beauty. But Nume's situation as Aphrodite in patriarchy is revealed when readers realize that kept isolated by her father before her marriage, Nume is the essence of a "gift" traded between patriarchs. In her isolation, she is patriarchally perfect, a maid (made) for male consumption.

Nume's "situation" is recognized by the American matron Jenny Davis who strives to educate Nume into the power aspects of Aphroditean feminine sensuality as a way to gain autonomy in this man's game of love. As an invocation of Hera (the archetypal Wife), Mrs. Davis understands Nume's untapped sensual power and attempts to free Nume from her patriarch's imposed imprisonment in order to instruct her in the ways of an American New Woman:

[Mrs. Davis] took a great liking to Nume almost at once, and the girl returned it. She would walk into Omi's house in the most insinuating manner in the world, captivate the old man with her wit and grace, and carry off Nume right under his nose, even though he had told her of his resolve to keep his daughter in seclusion until her marriage. [...] And when she was alone with the girl and out of sight of the old man, she would say, with a confident shake of her head: "Just wait, my dear; soon I'll have things so that you can come and go as you like." (67)

Mrs. Davis spends hours instructing Nume in English and in the ways of American women, as if in an attempt to draw out Nume's coquettish aspects. However, Mrs. Davis's protégée becomes more than a willing student and absorbs the instruction so much that only trouble can result as the romantic plot develops.

The trouble begins about halfway through the romance when a lover's critical mass is created at the meeting of Nume and Sinclair. Now marked with the hallmarks of a powerfully sexual Aphrodite, Nume's pure sensual power leaves Sinclair at the mercy of her beauty when he first meets her at Mrs. Davis's party: "She was dressed very simply in a soft white gown, cut low at the neck, the sleeves short to the elbows. She wore no jewels whatever, but in the mass of dense black hair, braided carelessly and coiled just above the nape of her neck, were a few red roses. [...] He could not have told what there was in her face that struck him so with the peculiarity of its beauty. Her nationality puzzled him. [...] Sinclair felt a strange, indescribable sensation as her little hand rested in his; it was as if he held in his hand a little trembling, frightened wild bird" (84–85). Nume is presented as if she has stepped down from Olympus itself, in her flowing white dress, accompanied by Aphrodite's emblems of roses and birds. Sinclair is immediately struck dumb by Nume/Aphrodite's charm and beauty and gives her his undivided attention throughout the evening—even at the expense of his fiancée, Cleo Ballard. Mrs. Davis recognizes the problems inherent in Nume's advent into Cleo's and Sinclair's relationship, but from this moment, the fate of the four lovers is sealed.

When Nume expresses a desire for Sinclair and tells Mrs. Davis that Sinclair has led her to believe that he is *not* engaged to Cleo, Mrs. Davis reminds Nume of her earlier instruction, saying, "that's only a way American men have, Nume. You must not believe them; and be very careful not to tell them you like them" (93). Using Jenny Davis to refer to the notorious habit of American men to philander with Japanese women and then leave them,

Watanna subtly balances her construction of the femme fatale to equalize her relationships between women, while also intertwining a commentary on sexualized race relations between men and women. Likewise, as a version of Aphrodite as pure love, Nume's innocence has initially protected her from the corrupt world of white men and their sexual appetites; however, Nume chooses to seize power and proceed on her own, with only her maid Koto (a former Geisha dancer) to guide her.

As the novel closes, Cleo is reunited with her "better half" in the form of Nume/Aphrodite when the two women meet in the closing chapter of this unlikely fable. The meeting, it seems, is a reconciliation between Aphrodite and Undine, one that establishes Aphrodite's supreme power and puts Undine "back in her place," so to speak. As Nume/Aphrodite says to Cleo/Undine, "You mos' beautifoolest womans barbarian—No! no! nod thad. Egscuse me. I *nod* perlite to mag' mistakes sometimes. I mean I thing' you mos' beautifoolest *ladies* I aever seen" (217; Watanna's emphasis). Nume's mispronunciation of "beautiful" and her linguistic slip referring to white women as "barbarians" in Japan are laden with the double entendres of "beauti—*foolest*" and "woman's barbarian"; hence, Nume/Aphrodite purposefully and finally labels Cleo/Undine as a foolish amateur incapable of the refined and complex aspects of love, and she is banished from Aphrodite's exotic queendom to return to America.

*Miss Nume of Japan* is a remarkable novel for its complex investigation of the trope of Aphrodite as a liminal figure. Set between the cultures of America and Japan, the novel carves out a stopping point in the cycle of femin(ine)ist fiction as it brings together two races and cultures in the union of Nume and Sinclair. In this aspect, it is both a modern and worldly novel, yet it is able to touch upon the utopian backgrounds of Demeter's world as it boldly investigates the complexities of race relations in a racist world. But as the story of Cleo and Orito reveals, race relations can never be simple—indeed, they can be deadly. As a result, Watanna's narrative is a cautionary tale for an audience of white readers who might, through their imperialist attitudes, tamper with or destroy the lives of others who are not like they are.

While Onoto Watanna's *Miss Nume of Japan* was her first novel in a career of examining race through fiction, Alice Dunbar-Nelson's fictional works—unlike her journalistic pieces—rarely directly tackle issues of race. As Elizabeth Ammons explains, "Dunbar-Nelson's refusal to write obvious race fiction was," a "conscious" choice for a "young writer [who] rebelled against using literature for bald social or political purposes" (*Conflicting Stories* 66).

Yet under the guise of "art for art's sake," Dunbar-Nelson's refusal to write fiction that used black dialect or slave settings was itself a highly political position. Ammons summarizes Dunbar-Nelson's position: "To her era's prescriptive demands based on race, Dunbar-Nelson responded with emphatic disobedience. She would not specialize in Southern black dialect; she would not use fiction to educate bigoted whites about the history and problems of 'the Negro.' They could learn those things somewhere else. She would express her pride in race and self by acting on her right as a free human being to create art as she saw fit, not as she was told to" (67). Ammons speculates that Dunbar-Nelson's highly political decision was akin to suicide for a young black woman writer who refused to conform to the racist fictional standards of her day. Her refusal to write fiction that adhered to the structures of "local race color," however, places her at the forefront of an emerging tradition of black women's writing embraced later by Jessie Fauset, who as Hazel Carby illustrates, "represented in her fiction a middle-class code of morality and behavior that structured the existence of her characters and worked as a code of appropriate social behavior for her readers" (167). So like Emma D. Kelley-Hawkins's work, Dunbar-Nelson's fiction can be described as reading suitable for a popular late-nineteenth-century audience of young white women, in that it was imaginative and moral, as well as suitable for young black women who also participated in similar reading experiences.

Gloria T. Hull also speculates that the absence of strong and obvious black characters in Dunbar-Nelson's work may have been a product of the white-dominated publishing society in which she found herself: "The predominantly white reading public had been conditioned to expect black fictional characters to be either tragic mulattoes or happy plantation slaves. Because she concocted stories that bore no relation to most black life, she skirted the problems that these stereotypes presented. Thus, it is well to remember that she is not writing out of an established black short-story tradition—especially not a black female tradition—but is in her own way helping to create one" (*Color* 53). While there was a canon of black women's narrative, it was often in the form of local color dialect fiction, which Dunbar-Nelson rejected as a form of discourse alien to black middle-class sensibilities. So like Onoto Watanna, Dunbar-Nelson manipulates popular cultural stereotypes and draws inspiration from her own social experiences as a woman who inhabits many worlds, and none at all.

In a world where skin color, class, race, and gender opened some doors and closed others, a light-skinned woman like Dunbar-Nelson, who was often able to "pass" for white, struggled with her liminal social position. Like the water-sprite Undine, who exists in the liminal position between sea and land, humanity and animality, mortality and immortality, turn-of-the-twentieth-century femin(ine)ist authors of color like Alice Dunbar-Nelson also exist in a "no-woman's land" between white and black, Victorianism and modernism, the nineteenth and twentieth centuries, the Angel of the House and the New Woman. Thus, it is not surprising that Alice Dunbar-Nelson's short novel *A Modern Undine*, written on the bridge of two centuries from about 1898 to 1903, features a complex exploration of a modern New Woman who exists in the symbolic form of an Undine.

Alice Dunbar-Nelson first achieved her literary reputation at the youthful age of twenty with the publication of *Violets and Other Tales* (1895). After this most feminine volume, Dunbar-Nelson published a book of sketches and short stories that explored the Creole traditions of New Orleans entitled *The Goodness of St. Rocque and Other Stories* (1898). But in spite of these solid works, Dunbar-Nelson's literary career is too often eclipsed by that of her first husband, poet Paul Laurence Dunbar. The celebrated, almost storybook marriage between Paul and Alice was brief and turbulent, and when Paul died in 1906, the couple had been estranged for a number of years due to Paul's absences and frequent literary engagements, his addiction to alcohol and heroin tablets, and Paul's physical and emotional abuse of Alice. Interestingly, *A Modern Undine* (c. 1900) was written during these tumultuous years; however, like her other longer works of fiction, this short novel was abandoned as a project for publication when Dunbar-Nelson neglected her fiction to turn instead to feminist activism and journalism after her husband's death.

Born and raised in New Orleans, Dunbar-Nelson was a descendant of Louisiana's *gens de couleur*, a class of mixed-blood free blacks. Because she was the child of an ocean mariner (possibly European) and a seamstress of black and American Indian descent, Dunbar-Nelson's choice to investigate a mythical figure is not surprising, as she would have been heir to a rich oral folklore tradition from both her mother's and her father's side. Dunbar-Nelson's love of the sea, possibly gained from her father, is recorded lavishly in her diary on the occasion of her fifty-fourth birthday:

> Does one have to record "thoughts"? The water! Luxurious, voluptuous, lovely. Lapping, caressing, loving my bare body—when I get

> way out and slip my bathing suit down and no one can see me naked. Yesterday, like the ocean, breakers, foaming over me. [. . .]
>
> But the water! I came here for it. Weeks I dreamed of it. Here it is. No inconvenience too great for the love of it—even these hot days when it was calm as a mill pond and none too clean—I could wait. Lovely, luxurious, voluptuous water. Howe was right when he spoke of drowning as "the gentlest death the gods gave to man." To float on and on and on into sweet oblivion. What a temptation. (Hull, *Give Us Each Day* 325)

Dunbar-Nelson's lyrical description of the water is fit for Undine herself, a description thoroughly explored in her short novel *A Modern Undine*.

In addition to her love of the sea, Dunbar-Nelson inherited an admiration for things mystical, mythical, and spiritual from her mother. As Hull explains in her introduction to *The Works of Alice Dunbar-Nelson*, "Her daily living envinced [sic] an awareness of meta-realms of experience beyond the visible world which was rooted in her mother's Obeah beliefs and enhanced by her own attention to the spiritual arts" (xlv).[5] Because Dunbar-Nelson was a woman who wrote on the cusp of modernism, her attention to the occult was not unusual, nor were occult knowledges uncommon for turn-of-the-twentieth-century New Orleans culture that fused a variety of mainstream and marginal religions into the daily lives of its inhabitants. In this sense, Dunbar-Nelson's occult fiction participates in what Mae Gwendolyn Henderson describes as "speaking in tongues" or the process of writing fiction where "black women must speak in a plurality of voices as well as in a multiplicity of discourses" (22) to access the multiple social discourses of race, gender, and class, which are internalized and experienced socially by the author. Through this multiplicity, Henderson explains, "black women's speech/writing becomes at once a dialogue between self and society and between self and psyche" (19). Hence, it is not surprising to find that Dunbar-Nelson's most experimental work of fiction examines the psychology of a fictionalized Undine as an aspect of myth.

As its title indicates, Dunbar-Nelson's *A Modern Undine* is a complex psychological portrait of an Undine, or in African mythology, she is "the mermaid, mumma, water mother," or "the spirit, the very heart of water" (Hausman and Rodriques 117). From the first lines of the novel, Marion is presented as an Aphrodite-like Undine:

> It was in the still quiet of a summer night that Marion met Howard. The sea surged at her feet in a low monotone of life and death. The heavens,

a deep blue bowl, glistering [sic] with white points of gems, bent over the earth in an embrace of enfolding tenderness. The night was full of a thousand sounds and a thousand silences. The sea sobbed, the crickets whispered, the crickets shrilled; a night-bird sang somewhere afar, heart-breaking notes that rose and fell with the cadence of the sea. Above the minor treble of the little feminine sounds, boomed the hoarse call of an alligator in the bayou, like the deep-toned bass motif in an organ fugue. There would come an instant hush over the clamor when the waves seemed to soften their tone, the shrill-voiced insects would be silent, and the bird and the bayou king let the reverberations of their notes die away into the forest. Some wave breaking against the pier with more force than the other would start the silence into sound again, and the trees and the water and the voices of the night would sing their songs aloud unto the white diamonds of the skies.

There was no moon, but the stars cast dim shadows on the ground, and the waves were aflame with phosphorus. It spread a sheet of silver to the horizon; it leapt in forked tongues from the dash of a wave against the breakwater; it crawled in sinister lines over the wet sand. (3)

These two opening paragraphs of *A Modern Undine* evoke the image of an oceanic environment that is maternal, sleeping, living, and breathing in the hours before Aphrodite's birth from the phosphorus on the sea. Not surprisingly, the novel reveals that Marion's mother lives on the shores of this sea world in Marion's childhood home, thus reinforcing the interconnected notions of motherhood and the sea.

Here, under the cover of darkness, Undine might have been created from the same phosphorus that created Aphrodite, but without the benefit of the more positive aspects of the golden sun and its dawn. Unlike Onoto Watanna's golden Aphrodites, the picture painted here is dark and silvery, malevolent almost, as the phosphorus crawls "in sinister lines over the wet sand" to gather itself together in the shape of an Undine on the beach where Marion is standing. She is safe to come ashore on a night with "no moon," as those who might be watching will never know she cannot cast her own shadow. As a metaphorical Undine, she is also a literal woman of color standing alone on the shore of a white supremacist patriarchy. Interestingly, Dunbar-Nelson's narrative technique of casting her scene at night echoes that described by Maureen Honey where the personification of night as female was a poetic strategy deployed by black women poets of the early twentieth century to transform it from "a setting of terror, a time when Black people were tormented by white vigilantes, into one of peace" (*Shadowed Dreams* 16). Honey explains that for these poets, "night [...] was a time when the objectifying eye was closed in sleep and the freedom to be at one with the soul could be safely enjoyed" (16). By invoking a specifically feminine darkness, Dunbar-Nelson's narrative obliquely creates a black feminine touchstone that transforms the patriarchal negativity of "blackness" (and all of its danger) to the more positive, complex ambiguities of a female principle, powerful and mysterious. Under this cover, then, Dunbar-Nelson's figure of Undine is inspired by feminine night rather than masculine day, thereby elevating the subaltern qualities associated with darkness and femininity—subjectivity, emotion, and dreams—above the traditional qualities associated with masculinity and light—objectivity, intellectualism, and rational thought. Hence, Dunbar-Nelson casts her Undine as inheriting the powers of the night.

The Undine in this narrative is Marion Ross, a Southern woman who meets and marries George Howard, a Northern businessman who falls in love with Marion despite her distant personality. The novel opens with Marion standing alone in the sea-garden, when her lovelorn preoccupation with the sea is rudely broken by her future husband Howard. Her few words, coupled with her longing pose, captivate Howard, causing him to be "very much in earnest" and "eagerly impetuous" (4) toward her. As an Undine, Marion is portrayed as an adept changeling, able to "surrender herself to his mood" (5). But Marion's actions during this first scene foreshadow her inability to completely embrace her form as an Undine. She loses her concentration during Howard's discussion, to withdraw "into herself suddenly, and to have become once more the 'strait-laced, high-bred young lady of a last century type' which Howard had mentally dubbed her when he had been presented to her" (5). Swept away by her beauty, Howard ignores Marion's metamorphosis, as "the mood of the night was upon him and he talked recklessly, like a man whose brain is loosed from its everyday thrall of commonplace into a realm of fancy and poesy" (5). With hardly an effort, Marion's power as Undine is absolute and "inflames" Howard.

Readers must remember, however, that Marion is a conflicted "modern" Undine, echoing some of the confusion confronted by Cleo in *Miss Nume of Japan*. In this sense, Dunbar-Nelson's narrative appears to tell the story of an Undine who is more concerned with returning to the sheltering arms of her mother (the sea) than with achieving a soul through marriage. Importantly, the first scene of the novel alludes to Marion's indifference to the Undine's traditional pursuit of a soul. As her conversation with Howard continues, Marion avoids a discussion of souls:

> "No wonder you Southerners have such poetic souls," he rambled on.
>
> "I don't talk of mine," she assented. He listened eagerly. He had been generalizing. She had struck a personal chord in the conversation that emboldened him.
>
> "You don't talk of yours because—because—" he bent toward her.
>
> "The music is beginning," she said indifferently, "We must go in." (5)

Marion halts this conversation because she refuses to talk about her soul. In Dunbar-Nelson's femin(ine)ist narrative of a modern Undine, the acquisition of souls by water-women appears to stand for their acquiescence to patriarchal control. In contrast, the water imagery that surrounds Marion throughout the story alludes to her wish to be reunited with the utopian feminine world of the sea.

What's more, Dunbar-Nelson appears to be rewriting Fouqué's tale of the water-sprite Undine in that Howard is given the title "Sir Knight" (8) by Marion's sister Emmie during her boisterous teasing of the couple. During the teasing, Howard proposes in jest to Emmie, but withdraws his proposal to present it in earnest to Marion, who again is shrouded in the imagery of the sea as she reacts in panic to the offer: "She sprang to her feet and threw out her hands with an appealing gesture. 'You mustn't,' she panted, 'you mustn't say that. I—I—you know, I don't like that kind of joking'" (11–12). As a modern Undine, Marion seems more interested in preserving her state not as an ensouled, married Undine, but as a kind of mythical "virgin martyr" who would choose death over patriarchal control through marriage. The text seems to point readers to this path, as in response to Marion's refusal Howard calls her a "little misplaced Priscilla" (12) alluding to the fabled Christian martyr Priscilla who was thrown to the lions for wanting to preserve her virginity.[6]

As if to lay this virginal imagery on the reader as thickly as possible, Howard refers to Marion as "a white lily in a garden of roses" (12), and later as a "cold, white lily" (27). The lily, a turn-of-the-twentieth-century symbol of sexual purity, is also a symbol for the virginal aspects of the Goddess (Walker, *Encyclopedia* 542). As Scott Cunningham explains, the lily, an emblem of Aphrodite's domains of the moon and water, is used magically for breaking love spells (141). Interestingly, by choosing the lily as Marion's love symbol instead of the rose—the rose being a symbol of both love and maternity—Dunbar-Nelson's narrative seems to be saying that the modern Undine rejects her need for a man; in fact, her union with him might ultimately destroy her or distort his progeny—a theme that reappears in women's later modernist narratives such as Edith Wharton's *The House of Mirth* and Djuna Barnes's *Nightwood*.

Unwilling to become a handmaid to patriarchy, yet lacking a solid women's community like those found in Sara Orne Jewett's *The Country of the Pointed Firs* or Emma D. Kelley-Hawkins's *Four Girls at Cottage City*, this modern Undine resists marriage even after she accepts Howard's proposal, watching the arrangements "with a curious noninterest" and holding herself "aloof" from the preparations (16). She "seldom speaks" of her fiancé, and "she was passive and acquiescent, but offered no suggestions, nor made any alterations in anything submitted to her for approval" as she "dutifully" submits "to the ordeal of dressmakers and seamstresses and milliners" (16). Finally, the preparations are finished, and "Marion, spirituelle in a mist of white tulle" (20), is married to Howard. Unlike her new husband, however, Marion does not relish the union, as when they kiss, Howard "noticed with a pang the quick compression of her lips as his own touched them" (21). Unlike old-fashioned Undines, Marion does not relish the patriarchal bonds of marriage, longing instead for her lost soul tied up in the great Motherly ocean. After the ceremony, Howard takes Marion to Edgewold, which is itself the very edge of the world for Marion, far from the loving maternal arms of the sea. Without the inspiration of the infinite waters, Marion becomes silent and withdrawn and a "habitual silence fell between them" (30) reminding readers of the folklore that tells of how some Undines sell their voice for two human legs when they emerge from the sea and need to walk (Wienker-Piepho 92).

Marion's grief is deepened with the arrival of Grace Weaver, who weaves not grace, but strife into Howard's and Marion's relationship. Although readers may be familiar with the Greek Graces of love and joy, they may not be aware that "Homer knew only one Grace, named Cale or Kale, perhaps a cognate of Kali" (Walker, *Encyclopedia* 351). The personification of "Grace" as "Kali" or the tantric goddess of death and destruction can be seen as a clever wordplay by Dunbar-Nelson, accurately describing the effect a young poor girl named Grace Weaver has on Marion's family. The destruction begins to play out when, while walking in town for exercise on a cold winter afternoon, newly pregnant Marion sees her husband arrive home early from the city, and she overhears two businessmen discussing Howard's departure from the station to Grace's house. Marion is jolted by this news, but she manages to hail a cab to take her home. The shock of hearing about her husband's affair is too much, and in her torment, the sea reaches out for Marion: "She remembered trying to go up the stairs before the darkness and roaring of the sea closed over her head, for before the outstretched hand of the butler could catch her, she had stumbled partly up the stair case, striking heavily against the newel post as she fell" (36). The marriage she did not wish to be in and the child she did not desire to bear come together with monstrous consequences—her child is born tragically deformed. Marion's crippled son becomes the overriding metaphor for her life away from the supportive community of women and from the sea. As Marion cries upon her initial examination of her child: "'You are like my life, baby,' she sobbed, 'maimed and warped and imperfect, and yet all I have'" (44).

Marion's life continues to spiral out of control when Howard comes to tell her that his company "went to pieces, all to pieces" (61) in the economic crash and that the authorities are looking to arrest him for embezzling funds. From here the novel quickly draws to a close, when Marion's marriage fragments as Howard sees his company go bankrupt and deserts his family, thus demonstrating the correctness of Marion's initial hesitation to marry him. Edgewold and its contents are auctioned off, and Marion returns to her Mother's house near her beloved sea. Fittingly, the novel completes its circle when baby Ross dies and Marion symbolically returns him to the sea: "'Bury him by the sea, Mother,' she said quietly when she was asked, 'perhaps it will sing to him the same songs it has sung to me, and he won't be so lonely without his mother's arms'" (71). Importantly, Marion's wish for her child is also her wish for herself as a misplaced, modern Undine.

Unlike *Miss Nume of Japan*, which is able to establish a tentative connection to Demeter's world through Aphrodite's graces, *A Modern Undine* signals another stopping point in the cycle of femin(ine)ist fiction that continues to chronicle the feminine journey in the patriarchal underworld. In Dunbar-Nelson's narrative, Marion as a modern Undine is isolated completely by her liminality. By the end of the novel, the death of her child and the desertion by her husband have left her neither a mother nor a wife. She is estranged even from her sister Emmie who closes the extant version of the narrative in a startled reaction to Marion's request: "Emmie raised her head and stared at Marion in surprise. It was the first time she had ever heard her sister express a love for the sea. 'I wonder what George would think of that?' she murmured to herself" (71). A metaphorical modern Undine, Marion's world has fragmented to leave her only the smallest space in which to operate, so she symbolically returns to her Mother's home on the shores of the sea. Unlike *Miss Nume of Japan,* which is able to establish a tentative connection with the sentimental world through Nume/Aphrodite's feminine graces, and to the feminist world with the power inherent in Aphrodite's confident sexual nature, *A Modern Undine* operates as a kind of modernist marker, locating the isolation felt by many women in Dunbar-Nelson's social position. Thus, the symbolic Undine of Dunbar-Nelson's narrative serves as a criticism—or a warning—of the troubles to be found in the modern woman's journey from the nineteenth-century maternal bower to the corrupt urban world of men in a new century. But this is also a white world, and women of color are, like Dunbar-Nelson's modern Undine, isolated as well within a white social sphere.

From Aphrodite's romantic exotic queendom in Onoto Watanna's *Miss Nume of Japan,* to the painful isolation of the modern Undine in Alice Dunbar-Nelson's *A Modern Undine,* Edith Wharton's *The House of Mirth* (1905) and *The Custom of the Country* (1913) show the paradoxes and possibilities of Aphrodite and Undine in the patriarchal underworld. Wharton's novels are narratives of a lone Aphrodite struggling to survive in a patriarchal world, cut off from her deep background of the feminine and female worlds. In contrast to the women of Emma D. Kelley-Hawkins's *Four Girls at Cottage City* who encounter together the world outside that of their mothers, Wharton's women are alone, left to their own devices to survive in the androcentrism of this "brave new world." In this context, Wharton's novels present two paths available to the twentieth century's modern Aphrodite or Undine who struggles against patriarchy's attempts to conquer and commodify her: Aphrodite in chains, refigured as a passive and powerless Andromeda of patriarchal pleasure in the character of Lily Bart; or Undine, unleashed on unsuspecting and unprepared men in the character of Undine Spragg. In *The House of Mirth,* Lily Bart's options are limited like those of Dunbar-Nelson's Marion Ross, but because Lily does not have access to the extrapatriarchal power of the Undine, her only option is to choose death over patriarchal control—in essence "finishing the job" that Dunbar-Nelson's Marion cannot. In contrast, *The Custom of the Country*'s Undine Spragg seizes the power of Aphrodite's form as Undine and not only survives, but flourishes.

One hallmark of Aphrodite is her ability to change into any form in order to meet her goals; however, as the new century gets solidly under way, patriarchy's power has limited the "acceptable" forms of women's roles to those that support only essential, passive, and sexualized notions of women. By tapping into the powerful allegories of a deposed Andromeda and a triumphant Undine, Wharton's novels disclose that unlike the femin(ine)ist utopias of Sarah Orne Jewett's *The Country of the Pointed Firs* and Emma Kelley-Hawkins's *Four Girls at Cottage City*, women's avenues of self-expression at the dawn of modernism have been truncated, cut off, and appropriated by men. Aphrodite has lost much of her magical and mystical power, and she has been cut down to little more than a comely, sexualized object who is expected to reflect patriarchal priorities, constantly changing to meet its social whims. As Elaine Showalter explains, a woman's only hope for survival in this situation is to become a "sociological chameleon," since her survival within this society depends upon how cleverly she can manipulate its rigid sexual stereotypes (*Literature* 11); but for women like Lily Bart, the personal priority of self-actualization seems to have passed by the wayside. Instead, her priority is survival itself.

Wharton's femin(ine)ist analysis of this "real world" stripped of sentimentalization and romanticization shows that under patriarchy, Aphrodite's power has been usurped: men have stolen her magical weapons, and as a consolation, she is given a mirror. Chained to this vehicle of patriarchal representation, Lily Bart's Aphrodite becomes Andromeda; thus, the feminist power of Aphrodite is shackled by patriarchy's sexualized image of women in its effort to deny their autonomy to create woman-identified "souls." From the opening pages of *The House of Mirth*, Lily is marked with Andromeda's chains: "She was so evidently the victim of the civilization which had produced her, that the links of her bracelet seemed like manacles chaining her to her fate" (9). What was once Demeter's woman-identified domain is now Zeus's world—the world of the fathers—where women are seen only as images of male desire. Readers may recall that in the classical myth of Andromeda, Poseidon's anger at her mother's boasts of her daughter's beauty causes him to devastate the land with floods and to send a sea monster to terrify ships until Andromeda is given up as a sacrifice to the monster. Chained to a rock by the sea, Andromeda waits helplessly until Perseus, returning from the Gorgon war with the head of Medusa, observes her predicament. Using the head of Medusa, Perseus turns the monster to stone and claims Andromeda as his wife. Like Andromeda, Lily is not a weak or ineffective character, but a female sacrifice to the caprices of patriarchal society that are out of her control. She is described as being "in bondage to other people's pleasure" (35) and as a "sacrifice" to the "laziness and selfishness" (347) of "a social order which had condemned and banished her without trial" (405).

Wharton's modern Aphrodite/Andromeda resists even her Perseus Lawrence Selden (whom readers cheer as the "romantic hero" of the novel) and his efforts to "rescue" Lily through marriage:

> What had brought him there but the quest of her? [...] He would lift her out of it, take her beyond! That *Beyond!* on her letter was like a cry for rescue. He knew that Perseus's task is not done when he had loosed Andromeda's chains, for her limbs are numb with bondage, and she cannot rise and walk, but clings to him with dragging arms as he beats back to land with his burden. Well, he had strength for both—it was her weakness which had put the strength in him. It was not, alas, a clean rush of waves they had to win through, but a clogging morass of old associations and habits, and for the moment its vapours were in his throat. (211)

Instead of centering her energies on marriage with Selden, Lily appears to be focused on achieving the "republic of the spirit" as signified through her insignia: "a grey seal with *Beyond!* beneath a flying ship" (205). Selden, however, misreads Lily's desire for the reason that he is consumed with his Persean desire to "take her away" (376); thus, Selden cannot understand Lily's clinging hope that she can live as a free Aphrodite and that she does not want to be "saved" by the gilded cage of marriage.

A metaphorical Andromeda, Lily wanders through life hoping to find an alternative to the chains of her proscribed ornamental role, and she has spent a lifetime attempting to dodge the monster of marriage. In the novel's opening scene, readers learn that she has already established a pattern of avoiding the padlocks of wedlock. Lily rationalizes her choice, saying to Selden, "I threw away one or two good chances when I first came out—I suppose every girl does" (11–12). Lily then proceeds to "throw away" additional chances during the course of the novel, including opportunities with Selden, Percy Gryce, and Simon Rosedale. Like Dunbar-Nelson's Marion Ross who is signified as "a white lily" (12, 27), Lily Bart's imagery is also strongly identified with the love-breaking power of the lily, as she, too, resists marriage (Cunningham 141). Through her behavior, Lily reminds readers of Aphrodite's liminal position between worlds—by always being a woman who is on the marriage market, Lily survives through her identity as neither a single woman nor a married one. Frances Restuccia reminds readers that "the suppleness even of indecision is preferable to the phallogocentrism demonstrated in *The House of Mirth* by one male suitor after another who attempts to capture, crystallize, or define Lily Bart" (224). Thus, Lily's modern Aphrodite is like Alice Dunbar-Nelson's modern Undine Marion who finds the pursuit of a soul through marriage to be unsatisfactory, because she always hopes for a more satisfactory option to her predicament. But made clear by the conclusion of *The House of Mirth*, a woman's rejection of her assigned position within the patriarchy leaves only the choice to accept a position *Beyond!* the order of patriarchal power—in Lily's case, that position is her death.

Lily is faced with what Sandra Gilbert and Susan Gubar describe as constant "reification as a charming and ornamental commodity" (*No Man's Land* 133). Through patriarchal eyes, this is the "strength" of a changeable Aphrodite-like Lily, or as Lily's mother explains, "People can't marry you if they don't see you" (46). But because Lily is a woman who has no real access to the patriarchal power of Zeus's world, she inherits neither economic independence nor a "soul," so she must marry a rich man and serve him by imaging herself in his reflection. Because Lily is beautiful, she has the *possibility* of attaining membership in the class to which she aspires. Selden asks Lily, "Isn't marriage your vocation? Isn't it what you're all brought up for?" (11). For Aphrodites like Lily Bart, there is no other option for survival in Zeus's world. As Selden's cousin Gerty Farish describes it, "A dull face invited a dull fate" (216).

As Aphrodite, Lily's beauty is "the nucleus around which [her] life was to be rebuilt" (44). In the *tableau vivant*, her beauty is based on Aphroditean artifices such as dresses, corsets, hairstyles, makeup, and especially her ability to appear elegant in the proper place at the proper time. In the *tableau*, "Lily was in her element" (174) as Aphrodite-who-must-get-a-man. As Reynolds's "Mrs. Lloyd," Lily is Aphrodite as a blank canvas presented to phallogocentrism. The *tableau vivant* is Lily's fleeting victory as Aphrodite willing to represent herself for men: "She had shown her artistic intelligence in selecting a type so like her own that she could embody the person represented without ceasing to be herself" (178). As Mrs. Lloyd, Lily is an image named and created by men—she is no longer Lily, but the image of the wife of the nebulous Mr. Lloyd, created by Reynolds and arranged by Paul Morpeth. Her Aphrodite here is overtly sexual, as noted by the "experienced connoisseur" in the person of Ned Van Alstyne who remarks, "Deuced bold thing to show herself in that get-up; but, gad, there isn't a break in the lines anywhere, and I suppose she wanted us to know it!" (179). As Mrs. Lloyd, Lily represents the most extreme form of Aphrodite as object—she is an image created by men for the enjoyment of men. Van Alstyne vulgarly notes, "Gad, what a show of good-looking women" (183).

The tragedy of Lily's Aphrodite/Andromeda is that she is destroyed in the double-cross of a culture that fosters women's dependence on men and then punishes women for that dependence. Gilbert and Gubar explain that in the telling of a woman's experience such as Lily's, the reader can see only "hints" of "an untellable tale of female power and guarded allusions to the alien language in which it would have to be told" (*No Man's Land* 132). After missing her chance at marriage with Percy Gryce, Lily walks with Selden at Bellomont, where the text suggests Aphrodite's possibility for femin(ine)ist rebellion: "There were in her at the moment two beings, one drawing deep breaths of freedom and exhilaration, the other gasping for air in a little black prison-house of fears. But gradually the captive's gasps grew fainter, or the other paid less heed to them: the horizon expanded, the air grew stronger, and the free spirit quivered for flight" (84). But Lily's rebellion is quietly crushed. When she has to work in the hat shop, she gives up all hope of bartering her way in Zeus's world through passive beauty.

As Lily's descent continues, the Graces, who are Aphrodite's attendants, are transformed into the Furies, who are Persephone's attendants during her journey through the underworld:

> Shuddering darkness closed on her. "I can't think—I can't think," she moaned, and leaned her head against the rattling side of the cab. She seemed a stranger to herself, or rather there were two selves in her, the one she had always known, and a new abhorrent being to which it found itself chained. She had once picked up, in a house where she was staying, a translation of the *Eumenides,* and her imagination had been seized by the high terror of the scene where Orestes, in the cave of the

oracle, finds his implacable huntresses asleep, and snatches an hour's repose. Yes, the Furies might sometimes sleep, but they were there, always there in the dark corners, and now they were awake and the iron clang of their wings was in her brain. . . . (196; Wharton's ellipses)

Lily is haunted by the image of the retributive Furies who pursue the symbolic matricide of Demeter's world. The image, however, is too much for her, as she cannot see past the monster of the "new abhorrent being" to which she found her true self chained. As Anja Salmi explains, "the Furies set the tone of impending danger and foreshadow Lily's tragic end. Society, the monster, is approaching to devour Andromeda" (71). Awash in a "sea of humiliation" (194), Lily struggles to "keep her head above water," so to speak, but the chains of her fate drag her deeper and deeper. Defenseless and alone, Lily is "an organism as helpless out of its narrow range as the sea-anemone torn from the rock" echoing the symbology of the coral pin in Sarah Orne Jewett's *The Country of the Pointed Firs*.

Lily's inability to "save her soul" through marriage to Selden may appear to the modern reader to be a lack of determination in her character, but as Rosyln Dixon explains, "Lily's choices are reduced to absolutes: she can survive by compromising the ideal, or she can honor the ideal by sacrificing herself" (218). Nevertheless, Lily's desire for the republic of the spirit *Beyond!* the patriarchal underworld threatens the structure of the patriarchal social order as well as its authority; thus, she will never be considered a suitable marriage subject. Lily's liminal position between the world of women and the world of men means that she is cast out—damned if she does marry, and damned if she doesn't. As Shoshanna Felman explains, a woman located outside of male societal power cannot be signified as an autonomous being: "To fulfill perfectly her 'Woman's Duty,' to play her role correctly in this theater of the identical, to recognize specularly and reflect perfectly [a man's] 'identity,' she herself must disappear: she has to *die* as Other, as a 'subject' in her own right. The tragic outcome of the story is inevitable, prescribed as it is from the outset in the very logic of [her] representation" (8; Felman's emphasis). Thus, the Reynolds dress Lily had worn at the *tableaux* becomes a death shroud in the next-to-last chapter of the novel (429), signifying Lily's death as ultimately a determined fate.

Surpassing the fate of Dunbar-Nelson's Marion, the sea closes in upon Lily, leaving her "without anything to which the poor little tentacles of self could cling before the awful flood submerged them" (431). Hence, Lily recognizes that she has virtually no hope of resignification in her restrictive reality. Once Lily faces the truth that she is unable to resignify herself to gain a place within society as an autonomous woman, she has to die. According to Gilbert and Gubar, "Lily's world has reduced her to a kind of dead letter, a signifier who signifies nothing in the society she inhabits, after death—and only after death—she does manage cryptically to rebuke the novel's 'negative hero' for his unmanliness. [. . .] Her author may be incorporating this dead heroine into an extended 'ghost story' of female desire" (*No Man's Land* 164). The "word" that "passed between" Selden and Lily is the untapped language of Lily's femin(ine)ist resignification. In a patriarchal world, Lily's feminist potential as Aphrodite is reduced to a "ghost story," of a drowned Andromeda for the reason that her desire for individual autonomy is silenced.

Although readers can never know if Lily's death was a result of an accidental overdose or purposeful action, the conclusion to *The House of Mirth* signals a change in the direction of femin(ine)ist fiction. As Cynthia Griffin Wolff concludes, "Until Wharton wrote *The House of Mirth*, no one had troubled to detail what it would be like to be the women thus exalted and objectified" (128). Accordingly, Wharton's close reading of women trapped in this position highlights one of the principal tenets of femin(ine)ist fiction, due to the fact that Lily's isolation is so complete that she chooses death over patriarchal control. As Candace Waid illustrates, Lily "dies in order to escape the underworld" (47). Fittingly, in her attempt to return to Demeter's symbolic domain, Lily chooses chloral (440) as the vehicle for her passing. According to Waid, "She casts her lot with the most gentle of the underworld figures, Chlora, the goddess of flowers. (Wharton, of course, identified flowers with women and ornament): Lily takes the chloral in the hopes of entering the green and floral world of Elysium that lies beyond experience" (48). Perhaps through her death, Lily has begun the journey back to Demeter's utopian world—but it is a journey on which readers cannot accompany her.

Like Onoto Watanna and Alice Dunbar-Nelson, Wharton also played with the myth of the Undine, for *The House of Mirth* and *The Custom of the Country* are two paths diverging into a forest of femin(ine)ist choice.[7] In one, Lily is the sacrifice; in the other, Undine resists becoming a "sacrifice" to "a lot of dreary frumps [who] have everything they want" (*Custom* 182) to become the definitive femin(ine)ist conqueror of the patriarchal underworld. As Gilbert and Gubar explain, Undine is "the ultimate survivor" in a "pecuniary society that destroys Lily Bart" (*No Man's Land* 146–47). In contrast to Alice Dunbar-Nelson's Undine, Undine Spragg Moffatt Marvell de Chelles Moffatt is a triumphant modern Undine who has learned to manipulate patriarchal power to create herself on her own terms. While Alice Dunbar-Nelson's *A Modern Undine* remains an incomplete portrait of a confused figure of Undine, Edith Wharton fleshes out a full illustration of the rapacious powers of the Undine in *The Custom of the Country*.

Drawing on images of the sprite Undine, Wharton marks her main character with sexualized images of her Aphroditean watery origins. Undine Spragg's headquarters—her bedroom—is "white and gold," "with seagreen panels and old rose carpet" (12), conflating Aphrodite's symbology with Undine's, inasmuch as she is elsewhere described as "Venus-Like" (55). Moreover, her mermaid imagery is strong. An account of Undine's initial meeting with her future husband Ralph Marvell is illustrated as if to describe a fisherman catching the nymph in his net: "They sat down together on the red damask sofa, against the hanging cloaks. As Undine leaned back her hair caught in the spangles of the wrap behind her, and she had to sit motionless while the young man freed the captive mesh" (43). Undine, however is not the passive "catch" men might make her out to be, as "the episode of the spangles" provides "the way to a graceful allusion" (44) for this woman who is always performing. Like a true Undine, Wharton's character of Undine is "fiercely independent and yet passionately imitative" (12), and male adoration "was incense to her" (73). Unlike Lily Bart's sophisticated Aphroditean and urbane beauty, Undine's physical description portrays her as if she had recently arrived from her sylvan home in the lakes and streams: "Undine's beauty was as vivid, and almost as crude, as the brightness suffusing it. Her black brows, her reddish-tawny hair and the pure red and white of her complexion defied the searching decomposing radiance: she might have been some fabled creature whose home was in a beam of light" (14).

Undine's story focuses on her use of the tumultuous relationship with her fourth fiancé (engagements to Millard Binch and a New York riding instructor did not result in marriage) or second husband Ralph Marvell as a hunting-ground for Undine to hone her manipulative survival skills. As an Undine whose career is to attach herself through marriage to a man, Undine Spragg's every moment is wrapped up in preparation and presentation. She spends time lolling in front of mirrors, combing her hair and practicing "ladylike" behavior (14). Even more so than Lily Bart, who masterfully manipulates her sexualized representation as Mrs. Lloyd in the *tableau*, Undine revels in the omnipotent power of her reflection in the mirror: "She stood up and, going close to the glass, examined the reflection of her bright eyes and glowing cheeks. This time her fears were superfluous: there were to be no more mistakes and no more follies now! She was going to know the right people at last—she was going to get what she wanted!" (19). In contrast, Lily Bart's doubts about what she sees foreshadow her ultimate end: "She peered at herself between the candle-flames. The white oval of her face swam out waveringly from a background of shadows, the uncertain light blurring it like a haze; but the two lines about the mouth remained" (*House* 36). Undine poses and practices in front of the mirror to perfect the right illusion—she "watches herself approvingly, admiring the light on her hair, the flash of teeth between her smiling lips, the pure shadows of her throat and shoulders as she passed from one attitude to another" (*Custom* 15). Therefore, Undine recognizes that her representation is her source of authority, and herein lies her power.

Ralph Marvell believes "his mission—the 'call' for which his life had obscurely waited" (52) was to shape and mold Undine into the proper image of a male-identified Aphrodite; however, he does not realize that he has stumbled onto Aphrodite in her "wicked" form as the fallen sprite Undine. As an Undine in the murky waters of the patriarchal underworld, Undine Spragg has no "soul," although she seems to be more occupied with attaining patriarchal power through marriage instead of the traditional Undine's task of attaining a soul through marriage. Unlike Lily Bart's Aphrodite-Andromeda who quietly fades from the scene, Undine Spragg's Aphrodite/Undine appropriates the patriarchal ambivalences inherent in her position and her power as a "wicked" creature to use for her own ends. Interestingly, Mary Daly describes "Wicked" as "beyond patriarchal 'good' and 'evil'" (100); hence, Undine accesses the power of her position as being in between the world of women and men.

While Marvell believes that Undine will bring him artistic power, he miscalculates Undine's ability to "throne over him" (212). Instead, he sees Undine as offering him a "freshness" and a "malleability" (51) for him to work with, and according to Marvell, "She was still at the age when the flexible soul offers itself to the first grasp" (51). Marvell's tragedy is that he truly believes that Undine is able to be fashioned in his image. After their marriage, he attempts to appropriate the power of patriarchal prerogative that defines women as empty vessels that need to be filled: "Her mind was as destitute of beauty and mystery as the prairie schoolhouse in which she had been educated [. . .]. The task of opening new windows in her mind was inspiring enough to give him infinite patience; and he would not yet own to himself that her pliancy and variety were imitative rather than spontaneous" (92). Marvell's downfall is that he misreads Undine's "pliancy and variety" as "spontaneous." In Marvell's version of Undine's development, she is signified as a magical, mythical muse who responds only to his male desire. The shades of meaning between Undine's "spontaneous" and "imitative" presentations are important, however, because they show Marvell misreading Undine as mirroring (imitative) instead of acting on her spontaneous need for power as a sprite. Under the cover of imitative behavior—that which is acceptable to patriarchy—Undine continually, yet carefully, shapes her process of image-making to stay one step ahead of patriarchal pitfalls in order to get what she wants. As Nancy Morrow explains, Undine "learns what to want; she imitates the desires of other characters, and these desires, in turn, guide her actions" (37). Undine is influenced greatly by the dictates of the social order as shown by "one of the guiding principles of her career: '*It's better to watch than to ask questions*'" (41; Wharton's emphasis). Thus, Undine quietly accumulates a kind of femin(ine)ist power, building it from power stolen right from under patriarchy.

Like Lily, Undine is initially positioned as Andromeda, but that image, too, is misleading. Ralph Marvell parallels Lawrence Selden on this point but with a distinct twist: "He seemed to see her like a lovely rock-bound Andromeda, with the devouring monster Society careering [*sic*] up to make a mouthful of her; and himself whirling down on his winged horse—just Pegasus turned Rosinante for the nonce—to cut her bonds, snatch her up, and whirl her back into the blue . . ." (52; Wharton's ellipses). Ralph, however, is "over his head," so to speak, as he underestimates Undine's "supernatural" (104) ability to simultaneously play and resist powerlessness. Thus, Ralph finds that Undine is no regular girl who needs rescuing. In fact, she is the antithesis of the weak, male-identified Aphrodite—she is a powerful Aphrodite/Undine in control of her own destiny. Undine is a femin(ine)ist "warrior Queen" (62) who strides through the patriarchal underworld as a splendid "Amazon" (77), whose machinations frustrate the male perspective that desires to read her as "Nereid-like" (90) or "Ariel-like" (95). Diametrically opposed to Lily Bart, Undine succeeds where Lily fails. Thus, Undine and Lily are two versions of femin(ine)ist existence under patriarchy, as they are "two halves of the same picture"—two extremes in one reality (Wershoven 72).

Eventually, Ralph's Pegasus is led astray (191), and Undine's Andromeda becomes a Medusa-like dominatrix who turns Ralph to stone (210), causing him to drown. As a kind of femme fatale, Undine gains power and autonomy through her embodiment of Mary Daly's *wicked* woman. By being blamed for Ralph's suicide, Undine is signified as the femme fatale who is positioned (by fearful patriarchy) in binary opposition to the virginal good woman of Lily Bart, when she is in actuality Lily's counterpoint. As Cynthia Griffin Wolff notes, "if Lily had simply decided to manage her career (instead of slipping into the comforting sleep of oblivion), she might have been like Undine" (239). Furthermore, critics sympathetic to Undine read her as redefining a "bad" position into something "good." For Ellen Dupree, Undine "is unwoman, the feminine essence that it is beyond the power of male thought to capture" (7). In short, while Lily's Aphrodite has had her power destroyed on the altar of male desire, Undine Spragg's Undine has seized male desire to use for her own ends, as she has mastered the Master's game and turned it to her advantage. As the character of Charles Bowen describes Undine, she is "a monstrously perfect result of the system: the completest proof of its triumph" (130). But although hers is a kind of self-actualization and form of feminist agency, those who are fearful of patriarchal retribution respond to the danger Undine's behavior raises for patriarchal control and reject her as one who is "out of hand," fearing the woman who is able to truly operate both within and outside of patriarchal control.

Undine's femin(ine)ist power lies in the fact that she rejects Aphrodite's passive aggressiveness for a determined and pugnacious agency to get what she wants. Because all is at her disposal, sometimes even herself, Undine has accomplished what should not be possible for women in the patriarchal underworld. Therefore, for Carol Wershoven, Undine is an interloper on patriarchy's plan to limit women: "With her capacity to become anything the buyer wishes, Undine soon sells what little selfhood she has to become whatever her lover and his world wishes. And, in transforming herself into the perfect commodity, Undine reveals the tawdriness of her men's desires and the essential cheapness of the world they inhabit. Rather than tempt her lovers away from their society, Undine invades it, triumphs in it, and thus exposes it for what it is" (71). Undine exposes that under patriarchy, women are faced with the opposing choices of death for "good" women or life for "evil madwomen," and she reveals that a woman's power lies in her ability to take control of the reflective mirror of patriarchal society. Through the double sexual power of Aphrodite/Undine she transforms patriarchy's double-cross of women into a femin(ine)ist double-double-cross of patriarchy itself.

Undine takes this control from the beginning of her story, as upon her arrival in New York, she immediately begins settling in on her quest for power, signified by her use of "pigeon-blood note-paper with white ink" (12). As one folklorist has noted, the pigeon is a more pedestrian form of the dove—the dove being one of Aphrodite's messengers of love and peace— and generally, pigeons are considered to be "greedy birds," and as such, they are an appropriate bird-sign for Undines (Zolar 292). Moreover, the conflation of the images of blood and breast milk signify the possibility of femin(ine)ist rebellion through a life that is possible when, as Hélène Cixous prophecies, "She writes in white ink" (251). Thus, Undine writes in what Gilbert and Gubar term the "alien language" of "female power," accessing the language of Lily's lost femin(ine)ist signification (*No Man's Land* 132). This imagery returns at the close of the novel in the scene of Undine's final triumph, or her marriage to Elmer Moffatt. Two of his wedding gifts to Undine at the end of the narrative are "a necklace and tiara of pigeon-blood rubies" (365). Moffatt, the man who was marked as Undine's most sympathetic mate by the symbolic "large imitation pearl" (63) he wore when they first met in New York at the opera, completes his symbolic and literal union with Undine by giving her the water sprite's favorite precious gem, the pearl, for Christmas. As Mrs. Heeny explains, "The necklace, which was formerly the property of an Austrian Archduchess, is composed of five hundred perfectly matched pearls that took thirty years to collect" (364).

Undine's ability to "write in white ink" marks her as providing an access to the unspoken feminist revolution of Lily Bart's *Beyond!* Appropriately, Grace Kellogg identifies Undine as Wharton's "strongest and most interesting heroine" (182). Undine Spragg as a metaphorical Undine resists her signification as Aphrodite created by men, and here lies her feminist potential; thus, Undine decenters her signification of Other outside of patriarchy to transform it into anOther femin(ine)ist power. Certainly, Undine's project employs a most feminist strategy, outlined by Luce Irigaray in *This Sex Which Is Not One* (1977) and one that Ellen Dupree summarizes as "a form of mimesis in which a woman deliberately exaggerates or mimics patriarchal discourse for the purpose of escaping its power to define her" (5). As an ever-changing figure, Undine eludes the patriarchal chains that attempt to bind and control her. Through her ability to reshape and reform herself according to patriarchal dictates, Undine provides a key to femin(ine)ist resignification.

Appropriately, Undine completes her narrative as a story of femin(ine)ist triumph. Instead of becoming an object for men to collect, she has become, like her husband, "the greatest collector in America" (363), accumulating power and wealth, as well as "items" from her previous marriages, including her son Paul and the de Chelles tapestries. More important, as a symbol of Undine's "Apex" of her achievement over the hierarchy of old European wealth, the Boucher tapestries parallel the Reynolds dress from Lily's achievement in the *tableaux;* however, while Lily ends her life "behind the social tapestry, on the side where the threads were knotted and the loose ends hung" (*House* 371), Undine ends her story thinking about the "clever stroke in capturing the Saint Desert tapestries" as she "give[s] herself a last look in the glass, saw the blaze of her rubies, the glitter of her hair" (*Custom* 370) and turns her thoughts to new conquests. By being always in motion, constantly looking ahead to a new triumph over the order of patriarchy, Undine ends her narrative, as Wolff explains, "perched at the edge of the abyss," but she is on a precarious ledge above the patriarchal underworld, where readers "do not yet feel the full force of terrifying descent" (243).

# 5

## Hekate's Queendom of the Damned
*Djuna Barnes's* Nightwood

✴ Djuna Barnes (b. 1892) is a member of the third generation of women studied here, known traditionally as the "Lost Generation," who were born on the threshold of the twentieth century and came of age during a time of unimaginably rapid social and technological change and widening class divisions. It was the generation that included H.D., Georgia Douglas Johnson, Nella Larsen, Zora Neale Hurston, Janet Flanner, Edna St. Vincent Millay, Winifred Bryher, Nancy Cunard, Zelda Fitzgerald, and Kay Boyle. These women grew up in a time that saw the first cubist exhibition in Paris in 1907, the Triangle Shirtwaist fire in 1911, and the implementation of the first moving assembly line at Ford Motor Company in 1913. As teens, they witnessed the difficulty of implementing the Progressive ideals fought for by their mothers and grandmothers, as Suffragists demonstrated, were imprisoned, and led hunger strikes from 1913 to 1914, and liberal leaders such as Margaret Sanger were imprisoned for their views and activism regarding sexuality. For this group, the experience of World War I created a generation of alienated young adults in a post-Awakening world who rejected the "old" ideas of their foremothers and lived to think differently about life. Moreover, the new military strategy of attacking civilians that caused the sinking of the *Lusitania* in 1915, the British blockade used to starve German civilians into submission, the senseless carnage of the Somme, and the flu pandemic of 1918 established a firm faith for this group in the philosophy of living for the moment because death seemed to be at every turn. Ready to cut loose in the aftermath of the Great War, they were further alienated as young adults by an upsurge in American conservatism that saw Prohibition, red scares, immigrant quotas, the peak of Ku Klux Klan activity, the Scopes trial, and the advent of the Great Depression.

From the narrative metaphor of Perseus and Andromeda used by Edith Wharton in chapter 4, it is now possible to complete the modern woman's descent into the abyss of the patriarchal underworld. As fin-de-siècle narratives that investigate the bipolar choices available to women—to fade into obscurity bereft of self-fulfillment, or to model themselves upon a masculine plan—Alice Dunbar-Nelson's and Edith Wharton's texts signal the point where readers begin to feel the full force of women's terrifying descent into the darkest places of the patriarchal underworld. In this context, the narratives of the characters Marion Ross, Lily Bart, and Undine Spragg reveal a shift in the way modern women must perceive patriarchy for the reason that they end their lives alone, trapped behind an androcentric social tapestry, or perched precariously at the edge of the abyss. Thus it is possible to understand the metaphorical journey begun in Demeter's garden by the young Persephones of Jewett's *The Country of the Pointed Firs* and Kelly-Hawkins's *Four Girls at Cottage City* now reaching deep into the patriarchal underworld of a new century, where men rule and male-identification reigns supreme.

As narratives that investigate the lives of women who must conquer or be conquered by the patriarchal underworld, the fictional accounts of Lily Bart and Undine Spragg uncover the paradoxical double bind of modernist femin(ine)ism that exists between an (impossible) imagined freedom and the isolation of women under patriarchy. In the cycle of femin(ine)ist revolution that is indeed a turning of Fortuna's Wheel, Djuna Barnes's *Nightwood* (1936) can be read as moving metaphorically from the chasm's edge glimpsed by Undine to an extended inquiry into the full force of woman's terrifying descent into the abyss—a very modernist project. One can view this in Barnes's *Nightwood* through a reading structured by the metaphorical invocation of the underworld goddess Hekate: companion of lost Persephone, ally of the grieving Demeter, goddess of the crossroads. Hence the allegorical evocation of Hekate continues the circle of the literary trope of Demeter and Persephone begun in Sara Orne Jewett's *The Country of the Pointed Firs*.

The subject of much critical scrutiny and theoretical production, Djuna Barnes's *Nightwood* remains a kind of *roman sans clef*, reminding readers that contemporary approaches to literature have difficulty grasping the meanings found within Barnes's artistry. As Mary Lynn Broe explains in her introduction to a recent volume of criticism on Barnes's work, *Nightwood* invites a continuum of complexity: "For Joseph Frank the novel's greatness lay in its modernist enterprise of 'transmitting the time world of history into the timeless world of myth.' As the great art novel of the twentieth century—a kind of epistemological romp on the figural plane—*Nightwood* invites theory construction as it has encouraged critics over the past five decades to ransack the literary canon for analogies; at various times, *Nightwood* has been called surrealistic, Eliotic, Dantesque, Elegaic, Fugal, Elizabethan, baroque, even Gothic" (7). At the very least, Djuna Barnes's *Nightwood* reveals the insufficiency of our own cultural myths with which we might apprehend Barnes's art. But while critics have appropriated all manner of psychoanalytic, biographical, and postmodern techniques to deconstruct Djuna Barnes's most famous and complex text, none has yet dared to pull the interpretative thread of occult witchcraft in her novel. By utilizing the more distant mythic figure of Hekate—*Macbeth*'s patron saint of witches—with which to analyze *Nightwood* and its central character Robin Vote, it is possible to unravel additional complexities from the threads of this perplexing text.

Barnes's attraction to gothic classical or occult figures such as Hekate is not surprising when one considers her childhood and early teen years. Barnes's grandmother Zadel, with whom she was exceptionally close, was a practicing spiritualist and experienced medium in the theosophical tradition of Annie Besant and Madame Blavatsky (Herring 43). (Herring notes that there is a good chance Barnes's grandmother may have known these women personally.) But while Zadel ruled over her extended family with an exuberant philosophy of occult spiritualism and free love, Djuna was too often put into family positions that psychically scarred her. For example, there is some question as to whether Djuna and Zadel were involved in an incestuous relationship, and Herring, Barnes's biographer, reports that Djuna underwent extensive physical and mental abuse at the hands of her father, who may also have allowed her to be raped at age sixteen (53). Barnes's biological mother, who was often powerless to intercede on her daughter's behalf, remarked to Djuna in 1936 that "You have condensed your agony until its [*sic*] pure platinum" (quoted in Herring 203). As a result of the violations of her youth, Barnes indeed may have felt that she was living in a dark, hellish world. Furthermore, her early history may have prompted her to keep the absolute facts of her youth shrouded in mystery, thus creating the distant and melancholy persona Djuna Barnes is known by today.

Like Djuna Barnes herself, Hekate is an enigmatic and often misunderstood figure, more spoken about than speaking herself. While she is known by contradictory forms, scholars agree that Hekate is the goddess of the moon, of night, and of mystery and insanity. What's more, Djuna's name itself evokes Hekate's nighttime realm. Barnes responded to an inquiry regarding the name "Djuna" in this way: "If the name means anything, it means *the light of the moon*, because my eldest brother, when an infant called the moon 'nuna.' My father, at that time, reading the novel 'The Wandering Jew,' by Eugene Sue (?), liking the Prince therein, called *Djalma* (Indian) (I think) put the Dj on to the *una*, and there you are" (quoted in Herring 319). As a ruling metaphorical figure for *Nightwood*, then, Hekate's presence is felt throughout the metaphysical landscape of the novel; indeed, it is felt in the novel's very title, of which Barnes herself wrote, "like that, one word, it makes it sound like night-shade, poison, and night and forest" (quoted in Plumb 211). Certainly, the symbol of Hekate references the darkness of night in which most of the novel's action takes place while simultaneously touching upon the mystery, insanity, and cultural damnation of *Nightwood*'s characters, especially that of its central figure *La Somnambule* Robin Vote.

As Demetra George describes the goddess, "Hekate is portrayed as a torch-bearing Moon Goddess who wears a gleaming headdress of stars lighting the way into the darkness of the vast past of our origins and the depths of our inner being" (139). Classically represented as armed with two blazing torches and accompanied by hounds, Hekate is a descendant of the Titans (her parentage is attributed to Perses and Asteria) who retained her authority over heaven, earth, and the underworld even after Zeus attained power (Tripp 261). Hekate's connection with the Eleusinian mysteries of Demeter and Persephone reveals the pain and violence of Persephone's experience in the underworld, for according to Robert Bell, "It was she who observed the abduction of Persephone and, torch in hand, accompanied Demeter in her search for her. When Persephone was found, Hekate remained with her as attendant and companion" (219). As Persephone's chaperone in the underworld, Hekate is the goddess who accompanies women lost in the physical and psychic darkness of patriarchy, reminding readers of the metaphor of Demeter and Persephone embedded in Jewett's work at the beginning of this femin(ine)ist cycle.

Using Hekate as a comparative lens with which to view both Djuna Barnes's artistry and her peripheral place in society as a member of the expatriate Lost Generation, Hekate's liminality is one of the most important qualities of a goddess who governs that space that is literally a no-man's-land. For Sarah Iles Johnston, the concept of the limen is intimately connected with Hekate:

> Every *Limen*—the threshold, the cross-roads, the gate, the frontier—is by definition detached from its surroundings. A threshold is neither inside nor outside of the house, a frontier belongs to neither country, the crossroads are the junction of roads A, B and C but also belong to none of them; liminal places, especially crossroads, offer varied options but not reassuring certainties. If the violation of a boundary and the accompanying disregard of limits threatens to bring on the chaotic disorganization or even the destruction of established areas, then the boundary itself must be regarded as a sort of permanent, chaotic Limbo; associated with neither of the two extremes it divided, it eludes the categorization and control applied to them—it belongs to no one. (25–26)

As a representational femin(ine)ist text, Barnes's *Nightwood* exists as its own kind of literary *limen* articulating the lives of those who exist on the thresholds of patriarchy. In this way Barnes's novel articulates the liminal person's estrangement from society: Guido Volkbein is the mythical wandering Jew who fraternizes with circus performers and the transvestite Dr. Matthew O'Connor; Robin Vote is the sleepwalking alcoholic who stumbles from lover to lover; Jenny Petherbridge and Nora Flood are two women in search of a solid social identity. But for all of its surreal comedy, the damned characters in *Nightwood* cannot escape the certainties of modernity. They are, as Dianne Chisholm explains, "haunted by modernity's destruction of past forms of life and its failure to create new ones" (184).

In this sense, all of *Nightwood*'s characters exist within the margins of society, at the three crossroads of community, history, and identity. They participate in lives that present varied options for living one's life in the patriarchal underworld; however, theirs are lives that are not "reassuring certainties." Indeed, *Nightwood*'s characters exist in a permanent chaotic limbo between race, gender, and society, yet remain associated with none, eluding social categorization and control. In terms of this literary metaphor, then, a Hekatean arrangement of these characters permeates the chaos of the novel, as no one character clearly surfaces as a "hero"; instead, Barnes uses a modernist viewpoint that distributes the narrative among her disjointed characters, reminding readers of George's description of Hekate's intellectual perception: "As she looks three ways at once, Hekate gives us an expanded vision whereby we can stand illuminated in the present and simultaneously see warning or promise of the future from the Great Above or call back the past from the Great Below" (143). Within *Nightwood* readers can look to the past with Baron Volkbein, peer into the dark corners of the present with Dr. O'Connor, or contemplate the future with Nora Flood and the Marchesa de Spada. But in the waking dreams of *La Somnambule* Robin Vote, readers can experience the emotional drama of all three.

Marguerite Duras reminds us that "The writing of women is really translated from the unknown, like a new way of communicating rather than an already formed language" (174). Using the usual and unusual structures of language, Barnes structures a femin(ine)ist narrative reality that simultaneously rejects and welcomes the dominant discourse. Her art is that of playing with androcentric language and literary law. It is another kind of women's writing; or as Luce Irigaray explains, "An *other* writing necessarily entails an *other* economy of meaning" (133; Irigaray's emphasis). This is *Nightwood*'s always already appropriated newly created discourse: a witch's brew of words, signs, and symbols that at once accept and reject patriarchal laws of discourse.

Like her literary sisters, Barnes was marginalized in multiple ways—because she was female, bisexual, and not traditionally educated; however, the marginalization of women like Djuna Barnes did not lead to a simple reactive response to their position. Instead of writing *against* the authority of historical, political, societal, and cultural experience, femin(ine)ist modernist women such as Barnes wrote *differently from* the androcentric literary culture in which they were immersed (Benstock, "Expatriate Modernism" 23). Alan Singer explains this narrative strategy further, stating that "Barnes's own metaphors are radically different from the metaphors of linear-representational narrative. Barnes's figurative language insists upon ceaselessly revising perspectives, substituting one identity among differences for another in an infinite process of emergent meaning" (67). In other words, Djuna Barnes did not allow herself to be bound by the laws of literary fiction that dictate metaphors and tropes be used in a certain way; instead, she borrowed—or transformed—aspects of popular and classical culture to fit her fictional needs in an expert application of T. S. Eliot's mythical method. Alicia Ostriker explains that this is a particular strategy of women's writing whereby a woman author "simultaneously deconstructs a prior 'myth' or 'story' and constructs a new one which includes, instead of exclud[es], herself" (316). Barnes, then, takes Eliot's mythic method one step further to create a radical femin(ine)ist narrative world within the space of traditional myth.

In its own way, *Nightwood* may have been the book written by Persephone as she suffered her exile from Demeter's world, isolated in Hades's domain. Moreover, Barnes's biographer writes that she herself "called her famous novel, *Nightwood*, the soliloquy of a soul talking to itself in the heart of the night" (Herring xvii). As if to illustrate this point, in her introduction to *Women's Writing in Exile,* Angela Ingram illustrates that exile for the women of Paris was not only a temporal reality, it was also a psychological reality. Not simply an act of resistance or a political rebellion, theirs was an exile from artistic community and the structures of patriarchal reality because they were not men. Moreover, Shari Benstock explains that for these women, expatriation had already been internalized through the actuality of their lived experiences under patriarchy, and that reality for women writers such as Djuna Barnes was "an exclusion imposed from the outside and lived from the inside" ("Expatriate Modernism" 20).

But exile for these women was not simply a termination of their struggle against its effects. Ingram explains that these writers carefully dissected the effects of their exile within patriarchy in ways that reached beyond their daily lives and into their artistry: "Displaced by official politics as well as by the political codes, both written and unwritten, of patriarchy, these writers exile themselves in ways that constitute subversion of political norms and of official versions of reality. In the process, they decenter notions of genre and text and consequently challenge and destabilize the reader's political certainties" (6). Femin(ine)ist modernist writers such as Barnes who were displaced by modern society occult that displacement within their artistic work, upsetting the expected relationship between reader and text. Thus, when the reader's "political certainties" are destabilized, her immediate response is to deny out of fear the tyrannical reality for women under patriarchy portrayed by the text; therefore, texts such as *Nightwood* remained marginalized under the traditional literary canon because they speak explicitly of these realities.

In a sense, Djuna Barnes has in *Nightwood* written her way into Elaine Showalter's "wild zone" ("Feminist Criticism" 262) of women's writing. In the fictional wild zone of *Nightwood* one can examine in detail the dystopian modernist experience foreshadowed by Jewett's Joanna fully illustrated in the lives of Robin Vote and her comrades. Like Joanna's story, the "untellable" woman's tale of *Nightwood* is experienced under cover of darkness. No longer the fantastic "idyllic enclave" (263) of Joanna's isolated island, the physical and emotional wild zone of *Nightwood* is instead a nightmarishly chaotic landscape that exposes the modern reality of Joanna's romanticized late-nineteenth-century existence. Lost and alone in an androcentric modern world devoid of the patriarchal mediation of sympathetic mothers or communal sisters, the women of *Nightwood* deepen the tragedy of Alice Dunbar-Nelson's Marion and Edith Wharton's Lily Bart, as they appropriately play out the uneasy end-game of this femin(ine)ist cycle.[1]

The indefinable qualities of liminal places cause fear for those who must transverse them, but not for Barnes's characters who live inside of them. Thus, Hekate is the perfect symbolic figure for apprehending the frightful world of *Nightwood* for the reason that she is the goddess who guides mortals across these liminal spaces; moreover, Hekate herself causes fear in her mysterious capacity to exist comfortably within a twilight that is neither day nor night.[2] Dr. O'Connor, himself a liminal creature of "French nights" (Barnes 71) who exists between man and woman, explains their situation to Nora Flood saying, "The very constitution of twilight is a fabulous reconstruction of fear, fear bottom-out and wrong side up" (70). Through his prognostications regarding the night—his "favorite topic, and one which he talked on whenever he had a chance" (69–70)—Dr. O'Connor becomes in *Nightwood* a kind of Hekatean high priest, interpreting the events of the night and giving voice to a muted goddess. Or, as Victoria L. Smith illustrates, "The doctor implies that the stories of the disempowered only get remembered in legend, which has the valence of fiction or myth, whereas the stories of the powerful get remembered as history, which has the valence of fact" (197).

Indeed, *Nightwood* is laced with all the hallmarks of good Greek myth, as a substantially dramatic and bloody event opens Barnes's novel with the birth of Felix, Baron Volkbein. After suffering a traumatic nighttime labor, Hedvig Volkbein dies, but not before experiencing "the clatter of morning horses in the street beyond, with the gross splendour of a general saluting the flag" (3). Here, Barnes structures the opening paragraphs of her novel so that the symbolism of Hedvig's leaving the feminine night and the female world of childbirth to die in the dawn of phallogocentrism—and her biting commentary on that symbolism—cannot be missed in the phallic imagery of the military man and his flag. Metaphorically overseeing Hedvig is Hekate, who is a guardian of women in labor in addition to serving as a goddess of death. Johnson explains in *Lady of the Beasts* that these responsibilities were assigned to Hekate as a result of undergoing a purification ritual that involved being present at a birth and visiting a funeral (160). So fittingly, Hekate's metaphor is invoked in *Nightwood*'s blood-soaked opening, reinforced through references to Hedvig's "rich spectacular crimson" bed (3), and through references to Hedvig's home that was furnished, in part, with furniture decorated with Hekatean imagery: "Three massive pianos [. . .] sprawled over the thick dragon's blood pile of rugs from Madrid. The study harboured two rambling desks in rich and bloody wood. Hedvig had liked things in twos and threes. Into the middle arch of each desk silver-headed brads had been hammered to form a lion, a bear, a ram, a dove and in their midst a flaming torch" (6–7). Referencing Hekate's mythological depiction as carrying a torch to light her way in darkness of the underworld, and as sometimes having three animal heads that "represented the amalgamation of totem-animals from her primordial past" (Farrar and Farrar 125), the Hekatean heraldry of the torch and goddess-linked animals on a blood-red background mark the Dark Goddess's territory in *Nightwood*.[3]

*Nightwood* is indeed Hekate's milieu, populated as it is with "the people of the underworld" (31). Framing the grim nights of the novel, Dr. O'Connor asks, "Listen! Do things look in the ten or twelve of noon as they look in the dark?" (73). A narrative that illuminates with a faint light the world of things that usually lie unseen, *Nightwood* reveals all to those who would only stay awake to experience it. Dr. O'Connor explains the process of the night in graphic detail, saying, "So, I say, what of the night, the terrible night? The darkness is the closet in which your lover roosts her heart, and that night-fowl that caws against her spirit and yours, dropping between you and her the awful estrangement of his bowels. The drip of your tears is his implacable pulse. Night people do not bury their dead, but on the neck of you, their beloved and waking, sling the creature, husked of its gestures. And where you go, it goes, the two of you, your living and her dead, that will not die; to daylight, to life, to grief, until both are carrion" (76). Thus Dr. O'Connor elucidates the vampirism of despair experienced by those who inhabit an empty modern society. In this way, *Nightwood* creates a Hekatean heuristic that plumbs the depths of a fractured Victorian consciousness to bring to the surface the chaos of the modernist unconscious, finding that action unleashes its latent desires, fears, and perceptions. Or, as Edward Gunn explains, "The novel draws the structure of its conflict from a conception of the mind in tension; historically and individually created in unknown, unknowable circumstances akin to concepts of Dionysian darkness, chaos, and formlessness, yet shaped unconsciously by a fusion of actual memory and given religious-cultural myths" (547). The central tension of the novel, then, is how to gather up this knowledge and put it back where it belongs. Unfortunately, the horrific genie of World War I and other traumatic early-century events has been let out of the bottle, so to speak; such is the essence of twentieth-century life experience. But while American society repressed these events into its national unconscious, the knowledge of these social traumas remained free in the dreams of its artists; and dreams, the vehicle of the unconscious, are governed by Hekate, who "stands at the crossroads of our unconscious" (George 146).

Hekate is most often imagined as a woman bearing a torch symbolic of her ability to illuminate the obscurity of the unconscious and is in her own way, *La Somnambule*. She is a figure "whose paradoxical function is to pierce that darkness, bring visions, call back the past, illuminate the present and give warning or promise of the future" (Farrar and Farrar 126). Hekate's association with the unconscious and with dreams reveals her power to terrify humans by sending them nightmares that might drive them to insanity, or conversely, to inspire them with dreams of creative inspiration. Demetra George explains that "As Prytania, the Invincible Queen of the Dead, Hekate dwelt in the underworld alongside Hades, Persephone, and other children of ancient Night—Thanatos (Death), Hypnos (Sleep), and Morpheus (Dreams)" (145). Accordingly, Robin Vote is inextricably bound with the figure of Hekate as she touches upon these three aspects of her underworld identity as death-maiden, sleepwalker, and dreamgiver. As deathmaiden, Robin can truly join her lovers only through death: "To keep her [. . .] Nora knew now that there was no way but death. In death Robin would belong to her. Death went with them, together and alone" (52). As *La Somnambule*, she moves through life with a "cataleptic calm" (42) and "like one in sleep" (44), but she is also "disfigured and eternalized by the hieroglyphics of sleep and pain" (56). As dreamgiver, she is for Leigh Gilmore "the simulacrum of the unconscious" who allows unconscious desires and knowledges to flow through her into our own experience (615). Robin's presence makes dreaming possible and meaningful, for Nora's dream demonstrates that "the dream had not been 'well deamt' before. Where the dream had been incalculable, it was now completed with the entry of Robin" (55). Robin as Hekate, guardian of the unconscious, allows Nora to see both backward and forward into her life, producing for her the realization that Robin is ultimately unattainable. Nora explains to Dr. O'Connor, "I can only find her again in my sleep or in her death" (109). In *Nightwood*'s reality, then, Robin becomes for other characters and for her readers a chaos of confusing responses that forces them to rely on reaction instead of rationality.

In this manner, Robin as a figure of Hekate haunts the three paths of our unconscious. John Opsopaus shows Hekate looks simultaneously "to the right, the sunny south, where the conscious mind reigns supreme and the unconscious is neglected; to the left, the north, cold and dark, where one wallows in the unconscious and conscious thought is slighted; and the middle way, toward a new dawn in the east" (n.p.). As Dr. O'Connor exclaims in his lecture to Nora, "We look to the East for a wisdom that we shall not use—and to the sleeper for the secret that we shall not find" (76), signaling to Nora that they are all Persephones exiled in an intellectual and emotional darkness where Hekate Robin Vote, broken by her modern condition, cannot pull herself together to share the secret of the way out. Appropriately, it is Robin's fractured and fantastical existence that simultaneously attracts us to her and repels us from her. She is a nightmare we do not wish to understand, thus we recoil from her in fear. But in order to really understand Robin, readers must remember Sigmund Freud's admonishment that "you must not blame the dream itself on account of its evil content. Do not forget it performs the innocent and indeed useful function of preserving sleep from disturbance" (143). Thus, Robin must sleepwalk through the patriarchal underworld because acknowledging her tortured reality will ultimately condemn her to the fate met by Wharton's Lily Bart. But in the figure of Hekate, Robin's dilemma also reminds us of the goddess's lunar power to give visions or to send madness. George explains Hekate's paradoxical power over inner knowledge: "The kind of understanding that this Dark Moon Goddess brings is not rational thinking, but it is more like the radiant suffused light upon which are borne the inspired visions of artists, dreamers, and seers. However, her light may bring more insight than a person can bear and result in chaos, shattering the illusions of the human mind. [...] Like hallucinogens to the underdeveloped mind, Hekate can poison as well as intoxicate and turn ecstatic inspiration into madness" (143–44).

Folklorist Barbara G. Walker explains that Hekate's intellectual lineage constructs her as a wise woman whose charge was to govern the power of words (*Encyclopedia* 378). As a governing trope for an analysis of *Nightwood*, Hekate's association with language is especially appropriate. For example, Shari Benstock argues that "an interest in language would seem to define the modern," and that "Modernism itself, seems to be about language—the history of words and the principles by which sentences construct themselves" (*Left Bank* 25). As a professional wordsmith, Djuna Barnes certainly had an interest in the construction of discourse and was sensitive to the polymorphic angles and layers of language. Her career as a writer began with poetry and touched upon nearly all the forms of written discourse—journalism, short stories, novels, and plays. Moreover, Benstock maintains that Barnes's work "consistently turns on classical sources of English words" (25); consequently, Barnes's interest in language, along with her childhood background in occult practices, reveals a well-read author who most likely would have been familiar with a wide range of literary narratives, including the characters of classical mythology and occult folklore. But unlike many of her modernist contemporaries, Barnes was self-educated, and, Benstock explains, she "learned etymology by reading the *New English Dictionary*" (25). In light of her experiences with spirituality and the occult, and as a self-taught etymologist, the careful craft of Barnes's writing takes in deeper dimensions of discourse: her education was self-paced, but it was also self-selected. She did not have to struggle against androcentric educational agendas; instead, she created her own femin(ine)ist interpretations and protected them through what Mary Lynn Broe describes as an "armor of etymology" (6).

In this context, *Nightwood* becomes a text that forges a Hekatean channel from patriarchal grammar to the glamour of femin(ine)ist knowledge that is simultaneously old and new, reminding us of Felix's description of Robin: "There was in her every movement a slight drag, as if the past were a web about her, as there is a web of time about a very old building [...]. So about the Baronin there was a density, not of age, but of youth" (101). In Robin, readers encounter a refiguration of silenced feminine experience, which

Smith explains, writing, "Robin embodies a kind of past that is not the historical past but rather the void of the past that must be filled with memory. More properly, then, she becomes a trope for memory, myth, remembrance" (200). In this sense, Robin Vote becomes a figure of a mystical woman who can, as Xavière Gauthier explains, "*make audible* that which agitates within us, suffers silently in the *holes of discourse,* in the unsaid, or in the non-sense" (163; Gauthier's emphasis). In the wild zone of *Nightwood* Barnes struggles to access a femin(ine)ist language with which she might refigure the verbal and intellectual silence of marginalized women, and where the creative use of language becomes an attempt to narrate a reality that exists within the *limens* of patriarchy. This task, however, is difficult and ongoing, because the reciprocity between the narrative (text) and the social (text) struggles to access the political dimensions of women's lives in the patriarchal underworld. It is not an impossible task, however, and this is the magic of *Nightwood*'s occulted allegory accessed through the narrative incantations of the femin(ine)ist writer. It is her attempt to literally spell out patriarchy's liminal spaces in her quest for an understanding and interpretation of modernist women's lives. But in order to undermine patriarchal restrictions on femin(ine)ist thought, this knowledge must be occulted within the layers of language, utilizing the power found in indeterminate meanings of words, and through the simultaneous evocation of the symbolic and the semiotic—a truly magical task.[4]

Through this narrative strategy, then, Djuna Barnes conjures a kind of femin(ine)ist incantation with her words; thus, *Nightwood*'s text is one that moves from the grammar of patriarchy to the glamour of femin(ine)ist knowledge regarding the patriarchal underworld. It is a truly *radical* enterprise, moving readers to the very root of meaning in the centers of individual words. For Barnes, this "Spelling Out Loud" uncovers femin(ine)ist knowledge from under layers of masculine imperatives. "Spelling," however, also indicates a witch's *spell,* the "words of a charm or incantation," especially in the sense of "witch" as "one who exercises transformative powers"; thus, Barnes's transformative power exists in her writing, which is often structured through a subversion of grammar structures and word meanings. In this context, Barnes's grammar is "glamorous"; it is not only mesmerizing, but also magical. This "Word Magic," then, creates a kind of grammatical "spell" (Daly 165, 180, 128). Its narrative structure and language are glamorous—ritualistic and primal—appealing to the femin(ine)ist reader's occult sensibilities about the power of Spider Grandmother's storytelling and the magic of her narrative.

*Nightwood*'s narrative disrupts the tyranny of patriarchal reality to focus for a moment on Hekate's queendom of the damned. In contrast to Wharton's Undine, who can be viewed as a triumphant queen of the patriarchal underworld, Robin Vote is the logical conclusion of toppling Undine from her patriarchal pedestal. Readers first encounter Robin as an interruption of a discussion between Dr. O'Connor and Baron Volkbein where significantly, Robin's chamber with its "red-carpeted floor" (34) and "the melancholy red velvet of the chairs and the curtains" (39) parallels Hedvig's apartment at the novel's opening. But while Hedvig seems to have been conceived of as a Hekatean handmaid, Robin appears to be cast from the figure of the goddess Hekate herself. In a sense, Djuna Barnes has drawn down the moon into the figure of Robin Vote.

Surrounded by symbols of the lunar goddess, Robin is encountered "On a bed, surrounded by a confusion of potted plants, exotic palms and cut flowers" (34). Plants were important symbols for the moon, and as Carl Jung explains, "The age-old belief that the moon promotes the growth of plants led in alchemy not only to similar statements but also to the curious idea that the moon is itself a plant" (132). Robin's alchemical description continues, fleshing lunar imagery into the form of Robin Vote:

> The perfume that her body exhaled was of the quality of that earth-flesh, fungi, which smells of captured dampness and yet is so dry, overcast with the odour of oil of amber, which is an inner malady of the sea, making her seem as if she had invaded a sleep incautious and entire. Her flesh was the texture of plant life, and beneath it one sensed a frame, broad, porous and sleep-worn, as if sleep were a decay fishing her beneath the visible surface. About her head there was an effulgence as of phosphorus glowing about the circumference of a body of water—as if her life lay through her in ungainly luminous deteriorations—the troubling structure of the born somnambule, who lives in two worlds—meet of child and desperado. (34)

Occult alchemists were fascinated with the union of opposites, or what Jung describes as the *mysterium coniunctionis* [the mysterious conjunction], and like T. S. Eliot who was always searching for a unifying myth that could hold all contradictions, ancient philosophical alchemists were fascinated with paradoxes and their resolution. In the character of Robin Vote readers are presented with that eternal paradox, and she functions metaphorically as an exotic moon-plant that might be the flora of immortality sought by mythic heroes, or she might be a lunacy-inducing poison plant that damns the taker to eternal madness. While the hint of "the odour of oil of amber"[5] that surrounds Robin might lead to an interpretation that she is indeed the key to immortality—for according to Walker "the basic word *amber* was a cognate of the Greek god's elixir of immortality, ambrosia" (*Stones* 90)—a contradictory passage a few lines later might produce the opposite interpretation: "she seemed to lie in a jungle trapped in a drawing room [. . .] thrown in among the carnivorous flowers as their ration" (34). Robin as paradox is constructed through dualisms: she is both "damp" and "dry," human and plantlike, "child" and "desperado," conscious and unconscious. This is Robin as Hekate, or the liminal woman who "lives in two worlds" (34), simultaneously participating in the worlds of body and soul, death and life, lightness and darkness, sleeping and waking, existing on both sides of the dualism without committing to one or to the other.

Further signifying her as a manifestation of the underworld goddess, Robin is described as having a kind of halo of "an effulgence as of phosphorus" about her head. According to Demetra George, Hekate is specifically marked by her unearthly glow: "In the legends Hekate has been described as a 'phosphorescent angel' that shines in the darkness of the underworld. This phosphorescence is the glow of death and decay. This is the hypnotic light of transformation (trance-formation), where the intrinsic nature of things is revealed through decomposition and renewal. Hekate symbolizes a kind of underworld consciousness of disassembly and assembly, which allows us to foretell certain kinds of catastrophic events because we are familiar with the signs and stages that precede the breakdown of form" (145–46). Supplemented by her phosphorescent glow, Robin's damp description presents her as Hekate pulled from the ground before her decomposition was complete. She is a woman trapped between death and life, thought and action, consciousness and unconsciousness.

Judith Lee touches upon this aspect of Robin, explaining Robin as "Calling to mind a moment that is preverbal, prerational, almost prehuman, a moment after death and before birth, Robin represents a consciousness which cannot be understood in terms of ordinary modes of differentiation" (215). Like Hekate herself, Robin causes her readers to experience a moment that remains outside of the boundaries of ordinary time, space, and language. As Felix describes her, "the Baronin had an undefinable disorder, a sort of 'odour of memory,' like a person who has come from some place that we have forgotten and would give our life to recall" (100). Nora, however, understands this as death, because she is, interestingly, more rigidly bound by social categories than the Baron (who remains acutely aware of them in his effort to manipulate them). In a sense, Nora seems to be aware that acknowledging and fully participating in the liminal space that is Robin will kill her self as she knows it: "Nora was informed that Robin had come from a world to which she would return [...]. Death went with them, together and alone; and with the torment and catastrophe, thoughts of resurrection, the second duel" (52). Furthermore, the Marchesa de Spada, an old hag "who believed in the stars" most firmly marks Robin as an otherworldly and extrapatriarchal figure, declaring "that everyone in the room had been going on from interminable sources since the world began, and would continue to reappear, but that there was one person who had come to the end of her existence and would return no more. As she spoke, she looked slyly at Robin" (62).

In order to make our way back to Demeter's garden, Opsopaus explains that patriarchal rationality should be abandoned, and that "we must become wild beasts, and make the Dionysian plunge into the waters of the collective unconscious" (n.p.). Robin begins that journey, for example, through her baptism into *Nightwood*'s underworld when Dr. O'Connor wakes her with a handful of water (35), paralleling in Robin's symbolic rebirth the literal birth at the beginning of the novel—it seems that in finding Felix unsatisfactory, the novel attempts to begin again with Robin Vote. Only by giving up the restrictive rationality of patriarchy and by abandoning herself to Hekate's instinctual animal leadership can this symbolic Persephone complete the cycle of death and rebirth that will ultimately lead her back to Demeter's garden. But with that submersion into the symbolic ocean of the unconscious comes the danger outlined by Heracleitus, who cautioned, "Sea water is the purest and most polluted: for fish, it is drinkable and life-giving; for humans, not drinkable and destructive" (quoted in Freeman 29). Thus, the knowledge Hekate—and Robin—reveals is ambivalent: it can both preserve and poison.

The symbolism of sea water's salt relates to Persephone's journey through the underworld and to Hekate's function as guide through the unconscious. As Jung explains, the alchemical attributes of salt are bitterness and wisdom, which also relate psychologically to one's ability to function in the world:

"Tears, sorrow, and disappointment are bitter, but wisdom is the comforter in all psychic suffering. Indeed, bitterness and wisdom form a pair of alternatives: where there is bitterness wisdom is lacking, and where wisdom is there can be not bitterness. Salt, as the carrier of this fateful alternative, is co-ordinated with the nature of woman" (246–47). In other words, sorrow is symbolized in the darkness of the new moon—Persephone has lost not only her guide, but also her way in the darkness of the underworld. In contrast, wisdom is symbolized by Hekate's light of the full moon, illuminating the wisdom gained from bitter experience.

The contradictions at play in *Nightwood* create a tension where the liminal becomes a space that needs to be played out, resolved, or synthesized; however, this is a desire that cannot be fully resolved at the novel's close. Nevertheless, the very construction of *Nightwood* begs the question as to whether or not this is possible. Traditional rules of narrative plot structure dictate endings that bring all the pieces of the novel's narrative puzzle together, however, Barnes chooses to follow her own rules that seem to mock the traditional rules of plot-driven endings. In a sense, Barnes (dis)closes *Nightwood* through what Rachel Blau DuPlessis terms "writing beyond the ending" whereby women writers invent strategies "that sever the narrative from formerly conventional structures of fiction and consciousness about women" (x). In order to produce a destabilization of traditional narrative structure, which is eventually played out in the final chapter entitled "The Possessed," Barnes begins building a fictional on-ramp to the metaphorical explosion that will happen in the space usually reserved for plot climax at the novel's close.

The groundwork begins to be laid in Robin's initial description where she is described as "a woman who is beast turning human" (36), with eyes that are like "the long unqualified range in the iris of wild beasts who have not tamed the focus down to meet the human eye" (36). The novel's attitude that Robin is "outside the 'human type'—a wild thing caught in a woman's skin" (121), underscores a modernist femin(ine)ist sensibility that calls for a turning away from patriarchal rationality in favor of the natural or bestial. Pulling Hekate's metaphorical thread, then, the beasts that populate *Nightwood* are emblematic of this process. At the Denckman circus, the animals "did not seem to see the girl [Robin], but as their dusty eyes moved past, the orbit of their light seemed to turn on her. [. . .] Then as one powerful lioness came to the turn of the bars, exactly opposite the girl, she turned her furious great head with its yellow eyes afire and went down, her paws thrust through the bars and, as she regarded the girl, as if a river were falling behind impossible heat, her eyes flowed in tears that never reached the surface" (49). Animals commune with Robin without words, reminding readers of Hekate's daughter Circe who had the power to transform men into beasts. Interestingly, like the inverted classical tropes used by Sarah Orne Jewett, Djuna Barnes also transposes classical allusion; here, she transposes Circe's ability to transform human to beast, and Robin functions as the beast turning human.

There is no speech in the last section of *Nightwood*, because just as Jewett's unnamed narrator ceases her literary production after her initiation into the feminine community of Dunnet Landing, participation in patriarchal language by the characters of *Nightwood* can only keep them trapped in the patriarchal underworld. "The Possessed" capitalizes on this trope as it plays out the symbolic consequences of ingesting the metaphorical pomegranate seeds of patriarchal language. In her effort to escape this painful destiny, Robin enters the chapel "as one renouncing something." She is "as one who hears of death suddenly," where "death cannot form until the shocked tongue has given its permission" (137). Robin is enveloped in silence, symbolizing her intention to reject the patriarchal underworld: "The silence that she had caused by her coming" is fractured only by the quiet sounds of insects and birds, but this is ultimately "forgotten in her fixed stillness" (138). Robin falls and is in pain, "but she did not call" (138).

In the scene at the chapel, "the night was well advanced" (138), alluding to both Hekate's nighttime atmosphere and the metaphysical darkness of the patriarchal underworld. Nora meets up with Robin in the chapel, and upon seeing her there, "Nora's body struck the wood, Robin began going down" (139). At this point, Hekate's dog greets Robin: "The dog stood there, rearing back, his forelegs slanting; his paws trembling under the trembling of his rump, his hackle standing; his mouth open, his tongue slung sideways over his sharp bright teeth; whining and waiting. And down she went, until her head swung against his; on all fours now, dragging her knees" (139). At the entrance of the dog, Robin moves fully into the no-man's land that Hekate's dog represents, and she begins her departure from the patriarchal underworld to go back to that "world to which she would return" (52) and "would return no more" (62).

This final scene in "The Possessed," however, stubbornly refuses to resolve the contradictions and paradoxes created earlier in the novel, and this is symbolized especially well by the dog in the chapel. As Buffie Johnson explains, "[Hekate's] own dog, named Cerberus, became guardian of the gate to Hades' realm. The dog assumes a shifting character, situated between night and day, or life and death" (117). On the one hand, dogs are connected to the goddess as lunar symbols of life that also protect humans from evil (114), but on the other hand, the dog's appearance with Robin casts her in Hekate's aspect as the death-goddess accompanied by her hound Cerberus, who would howl each time he saw a newly departed spirit who needed to be guided to a final resting place. Significantly, Nora's chapel is filled with the "howlings" of Robin, Nora, and the dog, each expressing deep feelings of loss. Thus, Robin is the "one person who had come to the end of her existence and would return no more" as predicted by the Marchesa at Jenny's party (62). She disengages from the patriarchal underworld to move outside of its morbid control and to return with Persephone to Demeter's realm.

But the unclear conclusion of *Nightwood* is mysterious and complicated, begging more questions than answering. Robin has opened the door to femin(ine)ist existence that reveals the way out of the patriarchal underworld, yet it is up to the reader to decide if she will make the complicated and difficult journey. But as Barnes's work shows, our Persephones in the fictions of Jewett, Kelley-Hawkins, Watanna, Dunbar-Nelson, Wharton, and Barnes must first find their way in the darkness of the patriarchal underworld to narrate a workable form of femin(ine)ist identity or be forever damned. Trapped in the game of predator and prey, they must delicately balance a fear of the unknown with a faith in the possibilities of unarticulated femin(ine)ist knowledge. To conduct themselves otherwise is to be marked as victims for patriarchal destruction.

# One Thread of Arachne's Web

\*  The limited scope of this analysis certainly shows that the territory of Arachne's tapestry is vast. While I have had the pleasure of running my intellectual finger along the course of one of her threads, it is difficult to appreciate the entirety of her artistry. To invoke a standard cliché, it is difficult to see the forest of femin(ine)ist fictions for Jewett's and Barnes's trees. Without fail, when the narrative patterns analyzed here of Sarah Orne Jewett, Emma D. Kelley-Hawkins, Onoto Watanna, Alice Dunbar-Nelson, Edith Wharton, and Djuna Barnes are held against late-twentieth-century feminist theories of language, they reveal a continuing struggle to access a femin(ine)ist language with which women might refigure the verbal and intellectual silence of marginalized women.

Could it be that these writers were on to something in their belief that women's narratives hold a kind of magical power? My study shows that the simultaneous use of a variety of theoretical approaches with a femin(ine)ist bent reveals the power of these texts through the abundant pleasures of critically intersecting with a text on a variety of levels—in order to take a childlike delight in playfully unlocking the secrets of a good book, or to admit that one's life has been radically transformed by reading a fictional tale. This is the very magic of narrative that consumes young people who *become* for days or even weeks the main character of the work they are reading. We need to remember that reading is *recreation,* or a re-creation of our selves, and it is through this re-creation that we can gain power, autonomy, and authority.

The texts that provide these kinds of experience for women—because not all texts will—offer tantalizing possibilities for a subversion of patriarchal language and for the liberation of women's words. But these texts also acknowledge the ongoing problem of the binary worlds and words of women and men. The solution for these authors, then, is to create a moment of being that exists on the thresholds of language and the fringes of texts. But the danger is that these liminal spaces are always in peril of being subsumed by encroaching dominant territory as patriarchy lays claim to own all that it is not and reshapes and reforms itself to accommodate that task. In other words, femin(ine)ist "wild zones" are always in danger of being tamed and domesticated; however, it is by their very multiplicity that these texts can resist patriarchal domestication to provide liberational sites for femin(ine)ist subjectivity.

So how can these texts unravel a thread that leads readers through the labyrinth of the patriarchal underworld to the true *Beyond!* of Lily Bart's utopian vision, or to Robin Vote's faraway world to which she can never return? Unquestionably, Robin has begun to open the door to reveal the way out of the harsh realities of the patriarchal underworld, yet it is up to the reader to decide if she will make that fearful and difficult journey with her. But as the works of these writers show, she must first find her way through the metaphorical darkness of the patriarchal underworld to find a workable form of femin(ine)ist identity or be forever damned—or dead. And the mythical method employed by these writers shows that the way out might be found in the dialectical spiral of works that shun linearity and synthesis for a cyclical philosophy of both/and that has room enough for contradictions.

The literature found along Arachne's web shows us that literary categories cannot be simple and clear-cut. They are intertwined and complexly related along a web of ideas that is lightly grounded at a number of intellectual anchor-points. It is significant that I close this study within the patriarchal underworld. Perhaps the modernist project of the early twentieth century was never completed, and the postmodern obsession with binary oppositions was simply a way of sidetracking us from what was truly revolutionary. It may be that only from our perspective in this new era can we look back to see what the modernists were really getting at in their all-out revolution.

Gloria Anzaldúa writes that "By creating a new mythos—that is, a change in the way we perceive reality, the way we see ourselves, and the ways we behave," we can create a new consciousness (80). Here, then, lies the most revolutionary aspect of the femin(ine)ist mythical method and how literature carries the magical possibilities for liberatory change—and of what Athena may have been most frightened. Myth, according to Milton Scarborough, "lays down a world in which theoretical enterprises subsequently become possible" (111). Perhaps, the theoretical threads of true liberation and Anzaldua's new consciousness are encoded in the worlds inhabited by the characters analyzed in the preceding pages. But while the apparatus for unraveling those threads are for now obscured from view behind Lily Bart's "social tapestry, on the side where the threads were knotted and the loose ends hung" (Wharton, *House* 371), the mythic method used by these authors points to their location in the darkness of the patriarchal underworld. In this case, "the nature of myth as giving expression to apprehensions of the life-world and as functioning to provide an orientation for living in that world" provides a pattern for lost women to follow as they struggle to make sense of the world they are now in (Scarborough 110). Only then can we complete the task begun by our literary foremothers.

# Notes

## Chapter 1. Mythic Methods and Femin(ine)ist Fictions

1. I have paraphrased the useful structure of this list from Brockway's *Myth from the Ice Age to Mickey Mouse*, 15.

2. *The Golden Bough* appeared first in two volumes in 1890 and finally in twelve volumes in 1911–15. Sarah Orne Jewett's *The Country of the Pointed Firs*, her third major work, was published in 1896.

3. There is, of course, a limit to my ability to do so and still meet the criteria for "scholarly" written work. My compromise, then, is to use the term "femin(ine)ist," while conceding that a wholesale redefinition of these terms is impossible to do in the limited space available here. I would, however, invite the reader to contemplate my new term's complexities.

4. In her essay "Volume Without Contours," Irigaray attempts to break down the hierarchical dualisms of male/female, in/out, mother/daughter, closed/open, singular/general, etc., to describe the power of the/a Woman that exists as an excess of these dualistic identities. As Irigaray explains, "she remains the whole of the place that cannot be gathered into a space because it is no more than a receptacle for the (re)productions of the same" (66).

5. In her essay "The Master's Tools Will Never Dismantle the Master's House," Lorde argues that it is only through a revolutionary break from patriarchy that genuine feminist change can occur. I believe, however, that we cannot create something out of nothing and that the "Master's Tools" are somewhat useful for dismantling the "Master's House." In other words, a hammer can be used both to build up and to tear down.

## Chapter 2. Occulted Words and Mythic Worlds

1. See Plumb's *Djuna Barnes' Nightwood: The Original Version and Related Drafts*

for a full discussion of the transformations the text underwent—ironically by T. S. Eliot—in order to make it "publishable."

2. Ordinarily, "occult" is synonymous with the practice of voodoo, demonology, sorcery, and devil worship, but in the terms of this study, occult will not focus on these practices nor on the magical phenomena associated with them. Instead, as mentioned above I will use "occult" as many modernists understood it: as that which is hidden from view, concealed, or beyond the realm of rational, logical comprehension. For other discussions of this topic, see Fraser's *In the Presence of Mystery*, Riffaterre's *The Occult in Language and Literature*, Kerr's *Mediums, and Spirit-Rappers, and Roaring Radicals*, Materer's *Modernist Alchemy*, Surette's *The Birth of Modernism*, and Greer's *Women of the Golden Dawn*.

3. Some believe America's so-called Greek Revival was established in the mid-nineteenth century when the Greek war of independence from the Turks recalled the American Revolution, and the archeological and architectural discoveries of the time sparked a renewed interest in the ideals of the golden age of Greece. Earlier, the War of 1812 had caused Americans to eschew all things British as well as Britain's fascination with ancient Rome (which had its roots in the late eighteenth century). This was an attitude fostered by American travelers who embarked on the "grand tour" expecting to venerate classical history, but instead formed a negative opinion of ancient Rome. As Kennedy explains in *Greek Revival America:* "The word *Roman* came to connote contemporary Rome and other crowded, plague-ridden cities. London was by then full of imperial Roman allusions, and hostile to Americans; likewise (and competitively), Napoleonic Paris had become a sort of fancy-dress stage set, where the First Consul had declared himself 'imperator' amid triumphal arches and columns that rivaled those of Trajan and Constantine. Americans who experienced all this pompous fuss developed an aversion to things Roman and a willingness to be convinced that Greek style was more becoming to a simple Society" (181). For nineteenth-century Americans, then, Greece and its classical history resonated with American democratic idealism and its break from Britain.

4. See, for example, Dijkstra's *Idols of Perversity*, Elliot and Wallace's *Women Artists and Writers*, or Honey's "Women and Art in the Fiction of Edith Wharton."

5. A quick survey of classical Greek myth reveals that the gods not only enjoy pleasure, but also patronize it through orgies of feasting, drinking, dance, and sex —behavior which was frowned upon by older American society, yet cherished by its youth. Greek myth also appealed to these writers as it provided explicit accounts of suffering and death: Sirens tearing apart men, children killing their parents, and lovers poisoning each other, as well as episodes of suicide and incest, spoke the unspeakable for writers who had themselves experienced the terrors of family violence or war.

6. Feminist literary scholars and others are beginning to analyze these allusions in studies such as Donovan's *After the Fall*, Ryder's *Willa Cather and Classical Myth*,

Sherman's *Sarah Orne Jewett, an American Persephone*, White-Parks's *Sui Sin Far/ Edith Maude Eaton: A Literary Biography*, Jay's *The Amazon and the Page*, or Hull's *Color, Sex, and Poetry*.

7. The impact of the shifts in populations due to mobilization for World War I, along with an extremely harsh winter in 1917, led to a flu pandemic that killed more than one half million in the United States. More than 62,000 American soldiers and sailors died of disease during the war, compared to 51,000 who lost their lives in battle. The battle of the Somme alone produced in excess of one million casualties.

## Chapter 3. Unraveling Demeter's Garden

1. Like the modernists of the first third of the twentieth century, Jewett and Kelley-Hawkins were circuitous regarding the psychological exploration of their characters. According to Wagner-Martin, a purposeful but discreet exploration of women's psychological responses to the trials of patriarchy characterized the texts of modernist women writers. In this sense, "less was stated, partly because women writers consistently disguised personal knowledge, and meaning was often caught in a symbol or an image" (13). Using this design to integrate femin(ine)ist knowledge through symbol and image, Jewett and Kelley-Hawkins knit together the occult strategies of disguise and displacement with the liberatory power of the word to create somewhat subversive, yet positive texts that mark them as precursors for femin(ine)ist modernism as they are foregrounded by the positive aspects of an insulating women's culture.

2. Although Donovan limits her study to white women writers, I propose that an attraction to and reworking of classical myth crossed racial boundaries. Without a widespread dissemination of Afrocentric myth in the popular culture of the time, women writers of color—like their white sisters—looked to cultural stories that were easily accessible in late-nineteenth-century American culture. These included, but were not limited to, classical and Christian myths. Moreover, these women were accessing the *American* culture in which they were raised. One's social position as African American or Asian American did not necessarily exclude the "American" part of one's heritage.

3. Blamires explains that the Tree Alphabet was used by ancient pagans for divination or for communicating secretly by placing tree leaves—each corresponding to a letter of the alphabet—on a wand, thus making the message incomprehensible to those who did not understand the symbolic system.

4. According to Walker's *Woman's Dictionary*, the wind was often the vehicle of the Goddess of the Voice. As Walker explains, "In biblical times, she was known as the divine afflatus, source of the prophets' inspiration: a personified Voice of God mysteriously female. Sometimes she was called 'the last echo of the Voice' meaning that there was not much left to be heard of the creative Logos" (329–30).

5. In reading Kelley-Hawkins's novel within the framework of the Demeter-

Persephone myth, I am not attempting to erase Afrocentric readings. Instead, I believe that Kelley-Hawkins's novel shows the complexities of women in the metaphorical "Persephone" role of a mother-daughter relationship. Similarly, when read from within the Greek Revival tradition of the late nineteenth century, it is possible to tease out the image of Persephone in *Four Girls* from both the girls' roles, and from that of the Christlike figure of Charlotte Hood, herself a resurrected figure as was Persephone.

6. During this time, many white Americans believed that black Americans were a "degenerate" and "inherently flawed" race that could never be assimilated into American society or act in a moral capacity. The case of *Plessy v. Ferguson* (1896) involved the constitutionality of a Louisiana law that required separate accommodations for white and "colored" passengers on railroads in the state. Homer Plessy, a citizen of Louisiana, had been arrested for refusing to obey the order of the conductor of a train to sit in the car designated for blacks. The court upheld the Louisiana law, denying that the law stamped blacks with a "badge of inferiority," suggesting that such would be the case only if blacks chose to put that construction upon it. Thus, *Plessy v. Ferguson* reinforced institutionally what black Americans had lived daily —the "Progressive Era" was one of the most racist and violent periods in America's history.

7. The notion of the "charm" is drawn from the Old English word "*Cyrm*, a hymn or choral song [. . . which is] a sacred incantation to the Goddess Carmenta, inventor of alphabets and 'words of power'" (Walker, *Encyclopedia* 162).

## Chapter 4. Aphrodite's Fall

1. The story of Aphrodite's manifestation as the sprite Undine is told in a number of children's stories: One tells of the water-sprite who marries a knight on condition that he shall never see her on Saturdays, which is the day of the week she resumes her mermaid shape. Adapting Paracelsus's story of the Undine, Friedrich Baron de la Motte Fouqué published the story "Undine" in 1812. Roughly, the story reads like a child's tale by Hans Christian Andersen and tells of the water-sprite Undine who is adopted and brought up by an old fisherman and his wife who had lost their own child. She meets the knight Huldbrand, who comes to the cottage; they marry, and Undine reveals she is not human. By marriage she gains a soul. Later, Huldbrand falls in love with Bertalda, who proves to be the fisherman's long-lost daughter. Undine returns to the sea, and when Huldbrand marries Bertalda, Undine returns to kill him with a kiss. Upon its publication, the story enjoyed international success; however, some in the American literary elite scorned the popular romantic tale.

2. Patriarchal mythmakers have worked hard to dismiss Aphrodite as simply the "goddess of love," or to dismiss her significance altogether. As Charles Seltman explains, "Of all the Twelve Olympians she is the most alarming and the most alluring,

so much so that many writers have tended to edge away from a discussion of her" (quoted in Friedrich 1). In fact, Aphrodite is much more complex than a simple love goddess, because she is also the manifestation of the virgin-mother-crone trinity of creator-preserver-destroyer (Walker, *Encyclopedia* 302). As the Goddess of Many Faces, Aphrodite might manifest herself in the form of Nemesis, the goddess of just retribution; or Fortuna, goddess of the wheel of time; or Androphonos, the Destroyer of Men. In this sense, she is more than a trivial goddess of love—her position as the goddess of sexuality was often feared by a masculine tradition that emphasized the primacy of her sister Athena (order and intellect). Certainly, Aphrodite's true power is a result of her various manifestations of female (sexual) power.

3. According to Ling, *Miss Nume of Japan* "has the distinction of being the first piece of imaginative literature in a broadly defined Asian American field" (*Between Worlds* 29). Eaton published thirteen novels and two fictionalized memoirs—two other novels attributed to Watanna have not yet been verified. For Doyle, *Miss Nume of Japan* is "A story of interracial love interspersed with Japanese scenery and shipboard travel, the novel established formulae that would win the author a substantial international readership" (54).

4. As Friedrich explains, "golden" is a special mark of Aphrodite, as "She is the most golden" of goddesses in the Pantheon as her special association is with the sun (78). Interestingly, as an epithet for Aphrodite, Friedrich clarifies "golden" as having deeper associations that relate it to speech and verbal creation, certainly a most fitting allegory for femin(ine)ist authors (79).

5. Loosely related to vaudou or "voodoo," Obeah "is a hybrid or 'Creolised' Caribbean religion with indigenous West African roots" (Richardson 5). A mystical oral tradition found in communities of mixed-blood and blended African peoples, Obeah was birthed in the slave communities of America and the West Indies. An amalgam of African, Caribbean, American Indian, and European folk beliefs, Obeah is enriched with a liberal dose of Catholic beliefs and traditions. Living in New Orleans, Dunbar-Nelson certainly would have encountered people, activities, and events that reinforced these beliefs.

6. Moreover, Priscilla is thought by feminist mythographers to be a Christian turning of the Mother Goddess—a conflation of Her with three virgin martyrs named Tatiana, Prisca, and Martina (Walker, *Encyclopedia* 817; Attwater, 330).

7. As McHaney explains in, "Fouqué's *Undine*," Wharton purposefully manipulated the popular narrative of la Motte Fouqué's mythological Undine: "Though Edith Wharton may have known several versions of the myth, it is quite likely that she had read the one by Fouqué. She handled her German well enough [. . .]. Even if she did not read Fouqué in the original, she would have found it available in English, because it was sufficiently popular to have been published in over sixty English-language editions prior to the composition of *The Custom of the Country*" (180–81).

## Chapter 5. Hekate's Queendom of the Damned

1. I do intend here to imply that there is more than one femin(ine)ist cycle. In *Nightwood*, I have chosen to complete what I see as the core of the web of femin(ine)ist modernism. It is necessarily a more negative emphasis here; in contrast, pulling the threads provided by Watanna or Wharton in *The Custom of the Country*, for example, might have led this inquiry along another path.

2. In this sense, mortal man's fear of Hekate may have come from her personification as Hekate Propylaia, or "the one before the gate" who offers protection from and governs the unknown of liminal places. See Robert Von Rudloff, "Hekate in Early Greek Religion" (7 July 1997. Horned Owl Publishing, 1996 <http://www.islandnet.com/^hornowl/library/hekate.html>).

3. See Johnson's *Lady of the Beasts*. Johnson details thirteen animals historically sacred to goddess worship, which include the animals listed in the selection above. It is my contention that Barnes specifically chose these animals for their association with the goddess.

4. Decoding these multilayered meanings becomes difficult in light of Barnes's self-education. For example, a resource such as the 1937 *Oxford English Dictionary* is useful in uncovering some of the multilayered dimensions of *Nightwood*, but because the influences of Barnes's occult interests and self-directed etymological education can never actually be determined, and because dictionaries are the "gatekeepers" of language and might miss some of Barnes's unorthodox etymological research, other resources regarding language need to be used to apprehend Barnes's text. In this context, Daly's *Intergalactic Wickedary* and Walker's *Woman's Dictionary* and *Woman's Encyclopedia* are examples of resources that have done much of the groundwork tracing the modern reconstruction of word etymologies and meanings through various language sources. What is more, the resources of Daly and Walker, of course, refuse to "bow down" (to pun on a chapter from *Nightwood*) to patriarchal definitions and may provide provocative feminist reconstructions of word meanings.

5. "Oil of Amber" is produced by dry distilling pieces of amber that are unfit for jewelry as well as dust and residues from the gem-making process. Amber oil is a dark amber clear liquid with a smoky odor similar to that of tanned leather. It was a popular perfumery ingredient before the rise of synthetic perfumes. By referring to amber as "an inner malady of the sea," Barnes may have been referencing the myth of the goddess Freya whose tears turned to lumps of amber when they fell into the ocean (see Walker, *Stones* 90).

# Bibliography

Ammons, Elizabeth. *Conflicting Stories: American Women Writers at the Turn into the Twentieth Century.* New York: Oxford University Press, 1992.

———. "Jewett's Witches." *Critical Essays on Sarah Orne Jewett.* Ed. Gwen L. Nagel. Boston: G. K. Hall and Company, 1984. 165–84.

Anzaldúa, Gloria. *Borderlands: La Frontera: The New Mestiza.* San Francisco: Aunt Lute Books, 1987.

Ardis, Ann. *New Women, New Novels: Feminism and Early Modernism.* New Brunswick: Rutgers University Press, 1990.

Attwater, Donald. *The Penguin Dictionary of Saints.* 3rd ed. New York: Penguin, 1995.

Baeten, Elizabeth M. *The Magic Mirror: Myth's Abiding Power.* Albany: State University of New York Press, 1996.

Bailey, Jennifer. "Female Nature and the Nature of the Female: A Re-vision of Sarah Orne Jewett's *The Country of the Pointed Firs.*" *Revue Française d'Etudes Americaines* 17.5 (1983): 283–94.

Baker, Michael. *Our Three Selves: The Life of Radclyffe Hall.* London: Hamish Hamilton, 1985.

Barnes, Djuna. *Nightwood: The Original Version and Related Drafts.* Ed. Cheryl J. Plumb. Normal, Ill.: Dalkey Archive Press, 1995.

Barry, Alyce, ed. *Djuna Barnes: Interviews.* Los Angeles: Sun and Moon Press, 1985.

Beauvoir, Simone de. *The Second Sex.* New York: Vintage, 1952.

Bell, Robert E. *Women of Classical Mythology: A Biographical Dictionary.* Santa Barbara, Calif.: ABC-CLIO, 1991.

Benstock, Shari. "Expatriate Modernism: Writing on the Cultural Rim." *Women's Writing in Exile.* Ed. Mary Lynn Broe and Angela Ingram. Chapel Hill: University of North Carolina Press, 1989. 19–40.

———. *Women of the Left Bank: Paris 1900–1940*. Austin: University of Texas Press, 1986.
Blamires, Steve. *Celtic Tree Mysteries*. St. Paul, Minn.: Llewellyn, 1997.
Bobo, Jacqueline. *Black Women as Cultural Readers*. New York: Columbia University Press, 1995.
Bradbury, Malcolm, and James McFarlane. *Modernism: A Guide to European Literature 1890–1930*. New York: Penguin, 1976.
Braude, Ann. *Radical Spirits: Spiritualism and Women's Rights in Nineteenth Century America*. Boston: Beacon Press, 1989.
Brockway, Robert W. *Myth from the Ice Age to Mickey Mouse*. Albany: State University of New York Press, 1993.
Broe, Mary Lynn. Introduction. *Silence and Power: A Reevaluation of Djuna Barnes*. Carbondale: Southern Illinois University Press, 1991. 3–26.
Brooker, Jewel Spears. *Mastery and Escape: T. S. Eliot and the Dialectic of Modernism*. Amherst: University of Massachusetts Press, 1994.
Caputi, Jane. "On Psychic Activism: Feminist Mythmaking." *The Feminist Companion to Mythology*. Ed. Carolyne Larrington. New York: Harper Collins, 1992. 425–40.
Carby, Hazel V. *Reconstructing Womanhood: The Emergence of the Afro-American Woman Novelist*. New York: Oxford University Press, 1987.
Chisholm, Dianne. "Obscene Modernism: *Eros Noir* and the Profane Illumination of Djuna Barnes." *American Literature* 69.1 (1997): 167–206.
Christian, Barbara. *Black Feminist Criticism*. New York: Pergamon, 1985.
———. *Black Women Novelists: The Development of a Tradition, 1892–1976*. Westport, Conn.: Greenwood Press, 1980.
Cixous, Hélène. "The Laugh of the Medusa." *New French Feminisms*. Ed. Elaine Marks and Isabelle de Courtivron. New York: Schocken, 1981. 245–64.
Clark, Suzanne. *Sentimental Modernism: Women Writers and the Revolution of the Word*. Bloomington: Indiana University Press, 1991.
Cunningham, Scott. *Encyclopedia of Magical Herbs*. St. Paul, Minn.: Llewellyn, 1996.
Cutter, Martha J. *Unruly Tongue: Identity and Voice in American Women's Writing, 1850–1930*. Jackson, Miss.: University Press of Mississippi, 1999.
Daly, Mary. *Websters' First New Intergalactic Wickedary of the English Language*. Boston: Beacon Press, 1987.
Davis, Thadious M. *Nella Larsen: Novelist of the Harlem Renaissance*. Baton Rouge: Louisiana University Press, 1994.
DeKoven, Marianne. "Gendered Doubleness and the 'Origins' of Modernist Form." *Tulsa Studies in Women's Literature* 8 (1989): 19–42.
———. *Rich and Strange: Gender, History, Modernism*. Princeton: Princeton University Press, 1991.
Dijkstra, Bram. *Idols of Perversity*. New York: Oxford University Press, 1986.

Dixon, Roslyn. "Reflecting Vision in *The House of Mirth*." *Twentieth Century Literature* 33.2 (1987): 211–22.
Donovan, Josephine. *After the Fall: The Demeter-Persephone Myth in Wharton, Cather, and Glasgow.* University Park, Maryland: Pennsylvania University Press, 1989.
———. "Sarah Orne Jewett's Critical Theory: Notes Toward a Feminine Literary Mode." *Critical Essays on Sarah Orne Jewett.* Ed. Gwen L. Nagel. Boston: G. K. Hall and Company, 1984. 212–24.
Doyle, James. "Sui Sin Far and Onoto Watanna: Two Early Chinese-Canadian Authors." *Canadian Literature* 140 (1994): 50–58.
DuCille, Ann. *The Coupling Convention: Sex, Text, and Tradition in Black Women's Fiction.* New York: Oxford University Press, 1993.
Dunbar-Nelson, Alice. *A Modern Undine. The Works of Alice Dunbar-Nelson.* Ed. Gloria T. Hull. Vol. 2. New York: Oxford University Press, 1988. 3–74.
Dunwich, Gerina. *The Wicca Garden.* New York: Citadel, 1996.
DuPlessis, Rachel Blau. *Writing Beyond the Ending: Narrative Strategies of Twentieth Century Women Writers.* Bloomington: Indiana University Press, 1985.
Dupree, Ellen. "Jamming the Machinery: Mimesis in *The Custom of the Country*." *American Literary Realism* 22.2 (1990): 5–16.
Duras, Marguerite. "From an Interview by Susan Husserl-Kapit." Trans. Susan Husserl-Kapit. *New French Feminisms.* Ed. Elaine Marks and Isabelle de Courtivron. New York: Schocken, 1990. 174–76.
Eliot, T. S. "Ulysses, Order, and Myth." 1923. *Selected Prose of T. S. Eliot.* Ed. Frank Kermode. New York: Harcourt Brace Jovanovich, 1975. 175–78.
Elliot, Bridget, and Jo-Ann Wallace. *Women Artists and Writers.* New York: Routledge, 1994.
Farrar, Janet, and Stewart Farrar. *The Witches' Goddess.* Custer, Wash.: Phoenix Press, 1995.
Felman, Shoshanna. "Women and Madness: The Critical Phallacy." *diacritics* 15.4 (1975): 2–10.
Fitch, Noel Riley, ed. *In transition: Writing and Art from transition Magazine, 1927–1930.* New York: Doubleday, 1990.
Fraser, Howard M. *In the Presence of Mystery: Modernist Fiction and the Occult.* Chapel Hill: North Carolina Studies in the Romance Languages and Literatures, 1992.
Freeman, Kathleen, trans. *Ancilla to the Pre-Socratic Philosophers.* Cambridge: Harvard University Press, 1948.
Freud, Sigmund. "The Censorship of Dreams." *Introductory Lectures on Psychoanalysis.* Ed. and trans. James Strachey. New York: W. W. Norton, 1966. 136–48.
Friedrich, Paul. *The Meaning of Aphrodite.* Chicago: University of Chicago Press, 1978.
Gauthier, Xavière. "Is There Such a Thing as Women's Writing?" *New French Feminisms.* Trans. Marilyn A. August. Ed. Elaine Marks and Isabelle de Courtivron. New York: Schocken, 1980. 161–64.

George, Demetra. *Mysteries of the Dark Moon*. San Francisco: Harper Collins, 1992.
Gilbert, Sandra M., and Susan Gubar. *The Madwoman in the Attic*. New Haven: Yale University Press, 1979.
———. *No Man's Land: The Place of the Woman Writer in the Twentieth Century*. Vol. 2. New Haven: Yale University Press, 1989.
Gilmore, Leigh. "Obscenity, Modernity, Identity: Legalizing *The Well of Loneliness* and *Nightwood*." *Journal of the History of Sexuality* 4.4 (1994): 603–24.
Greer, Mary K. *Women of the Golden Dawn*. Rochester, Vt.: Park Street Press, 1995.
Griffin, Jasper. *The Mirror of Myth*. London: Faber and Faber, 1986.
Gunn, Edward. "Myth and Style in Djuna Barnes's *Nightwood*." *Modern Fiction Studies* 19.4 (1973–1974): 545–55.
Hausman, Gerald, and Kelvin Rodriques. *African-American Alphabet*. New York: St. Martin's Press, 1996.
Hayes, Elizabeth T., ed. *Images of Persephone*. Gainesville: University Press of Florida, 1994.
Henderson, Mae Gwendolyn. "Speaking in Tongues: Dialogues, Dialectics, and the Black Woman Writer's Literary Tradition." *Changing Our Own Words*. Ed. Cheryl A. Wall. New Brunswick: Rutgers University Press, 1991. 16–37.
Henke, Suzette A. "(En)Gendering Modernism: Virginia Woolf and Djuna Barnes." *Rereading the New: A Backward Glance at Modernism*. Ed. Kevin J. H. Dettmar. Ann Arbor: University of Michigan Press, 1992. 325–41.
Herring, Phillip. *Djuna*. New York: Viking, 1995.
Honey, Maureen. *Shadowed Dreams: Women's Poetry of the Harlem Renaissance*. New Brunswick: Rutgers University Press, 1989.
———. "Women and Art in the Fiction of Edith Wharton." *Prospects* 19 (1994): 419–50.
Hull, Gloria T. *Color, Sex, and Poetry: Three Women Writers of the Harlem Renaissance*. Bloomington: Indiana University Press, 1987.
———. Introduction. *The Works of Alice Dunbar-Nelson*. Vol. 2. New York: Oxford University Press, 1988. xxix–liv.
———, ed. *Give Us Each Day: The Diary of Alice Dunbar-Nelson*. New York: Norton, 1984.
Ingram, Angela. "On the Contrary, Outside of It." *Women's Writing in Exile*. Ed. Mary Lynn Broe and Angela Ingram. Chapel Hill: University of North Carolina Press, 1989. 1–16.
Irigaray, Luce. "Volume Without Contours." *The Irigaray Reader*. Ed. Margaret Whitford. Oxford: Blackwell, 1991. 53–67.
Jay, Karla. *The Amazon and the Page*. Bloomington: Indiana University Press, 1988.
Jewett, Sarah Orne. *The Country of the Pointed Firs*. 1896. New York: W. W. Norton and Company, 1981.

Johnson, Buffie. *Lady of the Beasts: The Goddess and Her Sacred Animals.* Rochester, Vt.: Inner Traditions, 1994.
Johnston, Sarah Iles. *Hekate Soteria.* Atlanta: Scholars Press, 1990.
Jung, C. G. *Mysterium Coniunctionis.* Trans. R.F.C. Hull. New York: Pantheon, 1963.
Kaivola, Karen. *All Contraries Confounded.* Iowa City: University of Iowa Press, 1991.
Kelley-Hawkins, Emma D. *Four Girls at Cottage City.* 1898. Oxford: Oxford University Press, 1988.
Kellogg, Grace. *The Two Lives of Edith Wharton: The Woman and Her Work.* New York: Appleton-Century, 1965.
Kemp, Sandra. "'But How Describe a World Seen Without a Self?' Feminism, Fiction, and Modernism." *Critical Quarterly* 32.1 (1990): 99–118.
Kennedy, Roger G. *Greek Revival America.* New York: Stewart Tabori and Chang, 1989.
Kerr, Howard. *Mediums, and Spirit-Rappers, and Roaring Radicals: Spiritualism in American Literature, 1850–1900.* Urbana: University of Illinois Press, 1972.
Kristeva, Julia. *The Kristeva Reader.* Ed. Toril Moi. New York: Columbia University Press, 1986.
———. "The Revolution of Poetic Language." *The Kristeva Reader.* Ed. Toril Moi. New York: Columbia University Press, 1986. 89–136.
Lee, Judith. "*Nightwood:* 'The Sweetest Lie.'" *Silence and Power: A Reevaluation of Djuna Barnes.* Ed. Mary Lynn Broe. Carbondale: Southern Illinois University Press, 1991. 207–20.
Lindberg-Seyersted, Brita. *Black and Female: Essays on Writing by Black Women in the Diaspora.* Oslo: Scandinavian University Press, 1993.
Ling, Amy. *Between Worlds: Women Writers of Chinese Ancestry.* New York: Pergamon, 1990.
———. "Creating One's Self: The Eaton Sisters." *Reading the Literatures of Asian America.* Ed. Shirley Geok-lin Lim and Amy Ling. Philadelphia: Temple University Press, 1992. 305–18.
———. "Winnifred Eaton: Ethnic Chameleon and Popular Success." *MELUS* 11.3 (1984): 5–15.
Loeffelholz, Mary. *Experimental Lives: Women and Literature 1900–1945.* New York: Twayne, 1992.
Lorde, Audre. *Sister Outsider.* Freedom, Calif.: Crossing Press, 1984.
Materer, Timothy. *Modernist Alchemy: Poetry and the Occult.* Ithaca: Cornell University Press, 1995.
McDowell, Deborah E. Introduction. *Four Girls at Cottage City.* Oxford: Oxford University Press, 1988. xxvii–xxxviii.
McHaney, Thomas L. "Fouqué's *Undine* and Edith Wharton's *The Custom of the Country.*" *Revue de Littérateur Comparée* 45.2 (1971): 180–86.

Moi, Toril. "Feminist, Female, Feminine." *The Feminist Reader: Essays in Gender and the Politics of Literary Criticism*. Ed. Catherine Belsey and Jane Moore. Cambridge: Blackwell, 1989. 117–32.

Morrow, Nancy. "Games and Conflict in Edith Wharton's *The Custom of the Country*." *American Literary Realism* 19.1 (1984): 32–39.

Opsopaus, John. "Luna." *The Pythagorean Tarot*. <http://www.cs.utk.edu/mclennan/BA/PT/M17.html>.

Ostriker, Alicia. "The Thieves of Language: Women Poets and Revisionist Mythmaking." *New Feminist Criticism*. Ed. Elaine Showalter. New York: Pantheon, 1985. 314–38.

Plumb, Cheryl J., ed. *Djuna Barnes' Nightwood: The Original Version and Related Drafts*. New York: Dalkey Archive Press, 1995.

Restuccia, Frances L. "The Name of the Lily: Edith Wharton's Feminism(s)." *Contemporary Literature* 28.2 (1987): 222–38.

Richardson, Alan. "Romantic Voodoo: Obeah and British Culture, 1797–1807." *Studies in Romanticism* 32 (Spring 1993): 3–28.

Riffaterre, Hermine, ed. *The Occult in Language and Literature*. New York: New York Literary Forum, 1980.

Rosenblum, Robert, and H. W. Janson. *Nineteenth Century Art*. New York: Prentice-Hall, 1984.

Ryder, Mary Ruth. *Willa Cather and Classical Myth*. New York: Edward Mellen Press, 1990.

Salmi, Anja. *Andromeda and Pegasus: Treatment of the Themes of Entrapment and Escape in Edith Wharton's Novels*. Helsinki: Soumalainen Tiedeakatemia, 1991.

Scarborough, Milton. *Myth and Modernity: Postcritical Reflections*. Albany: State University of New York Press, 1994.

Schneider, Dorothy, and Carl J. Schneider. *American Women in the Progressive Era, 1900–1920*. New York: Anchor Books, 1993.

Sherman, Sarah Way. *Sarah Orne Jewett, an American Persephone*. Hanover: University of New Hampshire Press, 1989.

Showalter, Elaine. "Feminist Criticism in the Wilderness." *Feminist Criticism*. Ed. Showalter. New York: Pantheon, 1985. 243–70.

———. *A Literature of Their Own*. Princeton: Princeton University Press, 1977.

Silko, Leslie Marmon. *Ceremony*. New York: Viking, 1977.

Singer, Alan. "The Horse Who Knew Too Much: Metaphor and the Narrative of Discontinuity in *Nightwood*." *Contemporary Literature* 25.1 (1984): 66–87.

Smith, Victoria L. "A Story beside(s) Itself: The Language of Loss in Djuna Barnes's *Nightwood*." *PMLA* 114.2 (March 1999): 194–206.

Stoddard, Chris. *A Centennial History of Cottage City*. Oak Bluffs, Mass.: Oak Bluffs Historical Society, 1980.

Stroud, Joanne H. "Aphrodite and the Ensouled World." *The Olympians*. Ed. Stroud. New York: Continuum, 1996. 104–16.

Surette, Leon. *The Birth of Modernism: Ezra Pound, T.S. Eliot, W.B. Yeats, and the Occult*. Montreal: McGill-Queen's University Press, 1993.

Tate, Claudia. *Domestic Allegories of Political Desire: The Black Heroine's Text at the Turn of the Century*. New York: Oxford University Press, 1992.

Thomas, Gail. "Demeter." *The Olympians*. Ed. Joanne H. Stroud. New York: Continuum, 1996. 38–47.

Tripp, Edward. *Crowell's Handbook of Classical Mythology*. New York: Thomas Y. Crowell Company, 1970.

Wagner-Martin, Linda. *The Modern American Novel 1914–1945: A Critical History*. Boston: Twayne Publishers, 1990.

Waid, Candace. *Edith Wharton's Letters from the Underworld*. Chapel Hill: University of North Carolina Press, 1991.

Walker, Barbara G. *The Book of Sacred Stones*. San Francisco: Harper Collins, 1989.

———. *The Woman's Dictionary of Symbols and Sacred Objects*. San Francisco: Harper Collins, 1988.

———. *The Woman's Encyclopedia of Myths and Secrets*. San Francisco: Harper and Row, 1983.

Wall, Cheryl A. *Women of the Harlem Renaissance*. Bloomington: Indiana University Press, 1995.

Washington, Peter. *Madame Blavatsky's Baboon: A History of the Mystics, Mediums, and Misfits Who Brought Spiritualism to America*. New York: Schocken, 1995.

Watanna, Onoto. *Miss Nume of Japan*. Chicago: Rand McNally, 1899.

Watson, Carole McAlpine. *Prologue: The Novels of Black American Women 1891–1965*. Westport, Conn.: Greenwood Press, 1985.

Weigle, Marta. "Southwest Native American Mythology." *The Feminist Companion to Mythology*. Ed. Carolyne Larrington. London: Pandora Press, 1992. 333–61.

Wershoven, Carol. *The Female Intruder in the Novels of Edith Wharton*. Rutherford, Ill.: Associated University Press, 1982.

Wharton, Edith. *The Custom of the Country*. New York: Signet, 1989.

———. *The House of Mirth*. New York: Macmillan Publishing, 1987.

White-Parks, Annette. *Sui Sin Far/Edith Maude Eaton: A Literary Biography*. Urbana: University of Illinois Press, 1995.

Wienker-Piepho, Sabine. "Questing for Souls or Never Blame Supernatural Wives." *Nordic Yearbook of Folklore* 48 (1992): 91–104.

Wolff, Cynthia Griffin. *A Feast of Words: The Triumph of Edith Wharton*. 2nd ed. New York: Oxford University Press, 1995.

Zolar. *Encyclopedia of Sign, Omens, and Superstitions*. New York: Citadel, 1989.

# Index

African mythology, 68, 111n.2
Alchemy, 100, 102–3
Amazon, 83
Ammons, Elizabeth, 5, 6, 27, 32, 35, 65–66
Anderson, Hans Christian, 112n.1
Anderson, Margaret, 24
Andromeda, 7, 74, 88; in Wharton, 75–81, 83, 84
"Angel of the House," 32, 67
Anzaldúa, Gloria, 108
Aphrodite, 7, 15, 54, 55, 69, 73, 112nn.1, 2, 13n.2, 113n.4; myth of, 56–58; in Watanna, 59–65; in Wharton, 74–85
Arachne, 1–3, 106–8
Ardis, Ann, 4, 5
Asteria, 90
Athena, 1, 56, 108, 113n.2

Bailey, Jennifer, 29
Balzac, 21
Barnes, Djuna, 15, 16, 19, 106; inverview with Guido Bruno, 25; *Nightwood*, 72, 88–105; relationship to the occult, 89, 98, 114n.4; and spiritualism 23, 24
Barnes, Zadel, 89
Barney, Natalie, 16, 22, 53
Baten, Elizabeth M., 9

Beardsley, Aubrey, 21
Beauvoir, Simone de, 12
Bell, Robert, 90
Benstock, Shari, 93
Besant, Annie, 89
Blake, William, 21
Blamires, Steve, 32, 111n.3
Blavatsky, Madame, 24, 89
Bouguereau, Adolphe-William, 21
Boyle, Kay, 16, 20, 87
Bradbury, Malcolm, and James McFarlane, 18
Braude, Ann, 23
Brockway, Robert W., 7, 109n.1
Broe, Mary Lynn, 89, 98
Brooker, Jewell Spears, 8–11
Bruno, Guido, 25
Bryher, Winifred, 87

Campbell, Joseph, 7
Caputi, Jane, 2
Carby, Hazel, 66
Cassirer, Ernst, 7
Cather, Willa, 17, 53
Cerebus, 105
Charms, 51, 112n.7
Chavannes, Pierre Puvis de, 21
Chinese Exclusion Act, 53

Chisholm, Dianne, 91
Chopin, Kate, 17
Christian, Barbara, 43
Christian symbolism, 111n.2, 112n.5, 113n.6;
   in Kelley-Hawkins, 46–51
Circe, 104
Cixous, Hélène, 85
Cleio, 60
Coral, 40, 51, 79
Cottage City, 44–45
Couture, Thomas, 21
Crone, imagery of, 35, 47–48
Cronus, 56
Crosby, Caresse, 20
Cubist exhibition, 87
Cunard, Nancy
Cunningham, Scott, 72
Cutter, Martha J., 5

Daly, Mary, 82, 84, 99, 114n.4
Dante, 21
David, Jacques-Louis, 21
Davis, Thadious, 24
DeKoven, Marianne, 27
Demeter, 54, 65, 73, 75, 79, 93, 102. *See also* Demeter and Persephone
Demeter and Persephone, 7, 15, 55, 88, 90–91, 105, 111n.5; myth of, 30–31; in Jewett, 22, 30–41; in Kelley-Hawkins, 41–50; in Wharton, 22. *See also* Demeter; Persephone
Domestic novel, 42, 43
Donovan, Josephine, 30, 54, 111n.2
Dove, 85
DuCille, Anne, 44
Dunbar, Paul Laurence, 67
Dunbar-Nelson, Alice, 15, 17, 19, 53, 62, 80, 88, 94, 106; *The Goodness of St. Rocque and Other Stories*, 67; *A Modern Undine*, 58, 65–74, 81; relationship to spiritualism and the occult, 22–23, 68; *Violets and Other Tales*, 67

DuPlessis, Rachel Blau, 103
Dupree, Ellen, 84, 85

Eaton, Edith Maude. *See* Far, Sui Sin
Eaton, Winnifred, 58–59, 113n.3. *See also* Onoto Watanna
Eddy, Mary Baker, 24
Eliade, Mircea, 7

Far, Sui Sin, 17, 22, 53, 58
Faulkner, William, 58
Fauset, Jessie, 16–17, 53, 66
Felman, Shoshanna, 79
Femin(ine)ist, 58, 60, 67, 71, 75, 78, 85, 86, 105, 109n.3, 111n.1; ambivalence, 52; cycle of femin(ine)ist modernism, 14–15, 18, 28, 31, 37, 41, 42, 73, 88, 91, 94, 103, 114n.1; definition of, 12–14; language of, 36, 51, 80, 92–93, 98–99, 106–8; literary strategies of, 28–29, 45; relationship of, to mythical method, 13, 34–35, 108; strategies of, for women of color, 42, 43
Feminist language, 17–18, 106–8; relationship of, to femin(ine)ist modernism, 34; and word magic, 99–100. *See also* Language
Femme fatale, 62–63, 65
Fifteenth Amendment, 26
Fitzgerald, Zelda, 87
Flanner, Janet, 16, 24, 87
Foote, Mary, 26
Fortuna, 88, 113n.2
Fouqué, Friedrich Baron de La Motte, 71, 112n.1, 113n.7
Frazer, Howard, 20
Frazer, James, 7, 9
Free love, 89
Freeman, Mary E. Wilkins, 26
Freud, Sigmund, 7, 97
Freya, 114n.5
Friedrich, Paul, 56
Frye, Northrup, 7
Furies, 78–79

Gauthier, Xavière, 99
George, Demetra, 90, 92, 96, 97, 101
Gilbert, Sandra, and Susan Gubar, 27, 77–78, 80–81, 85
Gilded Age, 53
Gilded cage, 76
Gilman, Charlotte Perkins, 26
Gilmore, Leigh, 97
Glaspell, Susan, 17
*Golden Bough, The*, 109n.2
Graces, 72, 78
Great Depression, 88
Greek myth, 110n.5
Greek Revival, 110n.3, 112n.5
Green, Anna, 26
Griffin, Jasper, 21
Grimké, Angelina, 53
Gunn, Edward, 96
Gurdjieff, George Ivanovitch, 24

H.D. (Hilda Doolittle), 22, 87
Hades, 30–31, 36, 93, 96
Hall, Radclyffe, 23
Harper, Frances E. W., 26
Hayes, Elizabeth T., 31
Haymarket Riots, 53
Heap, Jane, 24
Hekate, 7, 15, 30, 114n.2; in Barnes, 88–105; in Kelley-Hawkins, 47–48; myth of, 90–91
Helios, 30
Henderson, Mae Gwendolyn, 68
Hera, 63
Heracleitus, 102
Homer, 21
Honey, Maureen, 69–70
Hopkins, Pauline, 26
Hull, Gloria T., 66
Hurston, Zora Neale, 87
Hypnos, 96

Imaginative realism, 30
Ingram, Angela, 93

Irigaray, Luce, 12, 85, 92, 109n.3

James, Alice, 26
Jewett, Sarah Orne, 15, 54, 104, 106; *The Country of the Pointed Firs*, 26–41, 48, 49, 72, 75, 79, 88; and spiritualism, 22, 27. *See also* Demeter and Persephone
Johnson, Amelia, 42
Johnson, Buffie, 1–2, 95, 104–5, 114n.3
Johnson, Georgia Douglas, 87
Johnson, Sarah Iles, 91
Joyce, James, 8
Jung, Carl, 7, 100, 102–3

Kaivola, Karen, 28
Kali, 72
Kelley-Hawkins, Emma D., 15, 54, 66, 106; and spiritualism, 27; *Four Girls at Cottage City*, 41–52, 72, 74, 75, 88; *Megda*, 42, 44, 46
Kellogg, Grace, 85
Kemp, Sandra, 13, 29
Kerr, Howard, 23–24
Kristeva, Julia, 17, 34
Ku Klux Klan, 88

Language: alchemy of, 19–20; in Barnes, 98–100, 104–5; magical safety of women's words, 29; and modernism, 98; patriarchal, 38, 40–41, 51; women's language and women's words, 38, 41, 51. *See also* Feminist language
Larsen, Nella, 16–17, 24, 87
Lazurus, Emma, 26
Lee, Judith, 101
Lévi-Strauss, Claude, 7
Lily, 71–72, 77
Liminality, 2, 56, 67, 73, 77, 79, 94, 99, 101, 103, 107; definition of, 91
Ling, Amy, 58–59
Lorde, Audre, 13, 109n.5
Lost Generation, 87, 91
*Lusitania*, 87

*Macbeth*, 89
McDowell, Deborah, 46
Mediators. *See* Patriarchy, mediation of
Medusa, 76, 84
Mermaid, 81
Millay, Edna St. Vincent, 22, 87
Modernism, 2, 68, 75, 96; characteristics of, 5; cycle of, 24–25, 74; relationship of, to occult, 20–25; use of myth in, 7, 20–22; and women's literature, 16–23, 49, 88, 91. *See also* Occult
Moi, Toril, 12–13
Moreau, Gustave, 21
Morpheus, 96
Morrow, Nancy, 83
Mother, 54, 56, 57, 60, 71; "Great Mother," 31; imagery of, 33, 35, 47, 72; Mother Goddess, 113n.6
*Mysterium Coniunctionis*, 100
Mythical method, 4, 93; relationship of, to semiotic writing, 17; relationship of, to women writers, 8, 10–11; T. S. Eliot's theory of, 8–11, 100
Mythology, 110n.5; relationship of, to ethnic heritage, 22; relationship of, to popular culture, 21; theories of, 7, 21–22; used by women writers, 4, 7, 22–25, 98

Nation, Carry, 26
Nemesis, 113n.2
New Woman, 42, 53, 55, 57, 58, 60, 62, 63

Oak Bluffs. *See* Cottage City
Obeah, 68, 113n.5
Occult, 89, 99; definition and use by women authors, 14, 19, 110n.2; relationship to modernism, 20–25. *See also* Modernism
Olympus, 64
Opsopaus, John, 97, 102
Ostriker, Alicia, 93
Ovid, 21
*Oxford English Dictionary*, 114n.4

Paracelsus, 112n.1
Patriarchal captivity, 54
Patriarchal control, 71
Patriarchal retribution, 39, 84
Patriarchal underworld, 32, 37, 45, 50, 51, 54, 80, 82, 83, 86, 88, 97, 99, 100, 104–5, 107
Patriarchy, 63, 69, 75, 90, 102; mediation of, 37, 38, 51; resistance to, 28, 70, 100
Pegasus, 84
Persephone, 54, 55, 56 93, 96, 97, 102, 103. *See also* Demeter and Persephone
Perses, 90
Perseus, 76, 88
Phelps (Ward), Elizabeth Stuart, 26, 50
Phrenology, 24
Pigeon, 85
Plato, 21
*Plessy v. Ferguson*, 42, 53, 112n.6
Pomegranate seed, 36
Popular culture, 4, 11, 14, 21, 22, 66, 93
Porter, Katherine Anne, 17
Poseidon, 75
Priscilla, 71, 113n.6
"Proclamation on the Revolution of the Word," 19–20
Progressive Era, 6

Race, 111n.2; in Barnes, 92; in Dunbar-Nelson, 65–67, 68; in Kelley-Hawkins, 45–46, 48; symbolism of, 46; in Watanna, 59, 65
Racism: in Kelley-Hawkins, 46; in Watanna, 62, 63
Radical, 99; definition of, 21
Redon, Odilon, 21
Restuccia, Frances, 77
Rose, 72
Rossetti, Dante Gabriel, 21

Salmi, Anja, 79
Sanger, Margaret, 87

Sappho, 21; in Millay, Barney, and H.D., 22
Scarborough, Milton, 108
Schneider, Dorothy and Carl J., 54–55
Scopes trial, 88
Semiotic, 20, 99; relationship to mythic method, 17; relationship to patriarchy, 17
Shelley, Percy Bysshe, 21
Sherman, Sarah Way, 31
Showalter, Elaine, 38, 75, 94
Sibyl, imagery of, 34, 35, 49
Silko, Leslie Marmon, 2–3
Singer, Alan, 92
Smith, Victoria L., 94
Social Darwinsism, 26
Society for Psychical Research, 23
Spencer, Anne, 53
Spider Grandmother, 2–3, 100
Spiritual feminism, 50
Spiritualism, 22–25, relationship to women's rights movement, 23
Spirituality, black women's, 41
Stein, Gertrude, 16, 53
Stoddard, Chris, 44
Stroud, Joanne H., 56
Subaltern, 70
Suffrage, 87
Surette, Leon, 20, 22
Swedenborgianism, 24

Tate, Claudia, 43, 45, 49–50
Thanatos, 96
Thomas, Gail, 31
Thought Woman. *See* Spider Grandmother
Titans, 90
Toomer, Jean, 24
Triangle Shirtwaist fire, 87

Triple Goddess, 40, 46–47, 60, 113n.2
Tubman, Harriet, 26
Twain, Mark, 59
Undine, 7, 15, 57, 58, 112n.1; in Dunbar-Nelson, 67–75; in Watanna, 60–61; in Wharton, 75, 80–85
Uranus, 56

Virgin, 71, 84; imagery of, 35, 72

Wagner-Martin, Linda, 111n.1
Waid, Candace, 80
Walker, Barbara G., 33, 34, 98, 101, 111n.4
Ward, Elizabeth Stuart Phelps. *See* Phelps, Elizabeth Stuart
Washington, Peter, 24
Watanna, Onoto, 15, 17, 22, 53, 66, 69, 80; *Miss Nume of Japan*, 58–65, 70, 73, 74. *See also* Eaton, Winnifred
Watson, Carole, 44
Weigle, Marta, 2
Wells-Barnett, Ida B., 53
Wershoven, Carol, 84
Wharton, Edith, 5, 15, 16, 53, 62, 88, 94, 97, 100, 106; *The Custom of the Country*, 58, 74; *The House of Mirth*, 58, 72, 74–81; and spiritualism, 23
"Wild zone," 107; in Barnes, 94, 99; in Jewett, 38–40; in Kelley-Hawkins, 49
Wolff, Cynthia Griffin, 80, 84
Woodhull, Victoria, 26, 55
World War I, 87, 96, 111n.7

Yezierska, Anzia, 17

Zeus, 30, 75, 77, 78, 90

Kristin M. Mapel Bloomberg holds the Hamline University Chair in the Humanities and is director of the Women's Studies Program at Hamline University, St. Paul, Minnesota. She specializes in American women's literature and culture of the late nineteenth and early twentieth centuries, with interests in feminist theory.

www.ingramcontent.com/pod-product-compliance
Lightning Source LLC
Chambersburg PA
CBHW020936230426
43666CB00008B/1698